August Zang

and the

French Croissant

How Viennoiserie Came to France

Jim Chevallier

Second Edition
Chez Jim Books ♦ North Hollywood, CA

First published 2009
2nd edition, copyright © Jim Chevallier 2009

All rights reserved. Without limiting the rights under copyrights reserved above, no part of this publication may be reproduced, stored in or introduced into a retrieval system, or transmitted, in any form or by any means (electronic, mechanical, photocopying, recording or otherwise), without the prior written permission of the copyright owner.

Published by:
Chez Jim Books

To contact, e-mail: jimchev@chezjim.com
or visit www.chezjim.com for the latest contact information

ISBN 9781448667840

Although the editor and publisher have made every effort to ensure the accuracy and completeness of these translations and any additional information contained in this book, we assume no responsibility for errors, inaccuracies, omissions, or any inconsistency herein.

Table of Contents

August Zang and the French Croissant..1
The Kipfel..3
Croissant Myths..9
    The Siege of Vienna...9
    Marie-Antoinette...11
    Enter, The Croissant 13
August Zang, "Baker"...15
    The Boulangerie Viennoise...16
    Innovations..30
    Zang's Influence..37
    Elegance and Upgrades...39
    The Baguette...43
Towards the Modern Croissant..51
The Father of the Daily Vienna Press..55
    Girardin...56
    Die Presse...57
    Zang, the Man 60
    After Die Presse...63
    "The Well-Bread Count"..64
Meanwhile, Back in Paris..69

*

ACKNOWLEDGEMENTS

I would like to express my thanks to *Die Presse* and in particular Monika Prüller of that publication's Press Archive service for their help with this work.

I am grateful too to Rudy Valtiner for use of his picture of August Zang's tomb.

*

ABOUT THE SECOND EDITION

This second edition includes a closer look at the rue de Richelieu in the nineteenth century and at Viennese baked goods in general, an expanded analysis of Zang's innovations and influence, a glance at the changes in bakery decor and revised overviews of the baguette and the changes in the croissant, as well as additional mentions of Zang in the American press.

*

A NOTE ON THE NOTES

Even academic readers may be dismayed to encounter over 200 footnotes in what is after all a very brief work. Though it has been tempting to leave what is often a colorful tale uncluttered, this book has its genesis in unsupported assertions about the croissant and other aspects of food history. Further, much of the information presented here is particularly obscure and scattered. This being the case, it seemed wiser to err on the side of a certain fastidiousness in identifying sources, for which I nonetheless beg the reader's indulgence.

*

August Zang and the French Croissant

How many readers over the years have sat with a croissant in one hand and their cheap, yet treasured, daily paper in the other? One man brought the first of these to France—from where it has since spread around the world—, then returned to Austria to introduce the second.

Though August Zang did not invent the croissant nor the cheap daily— any more than Henry Ford invented the automobile or even the assembly line—, he played a key role in introducing both. More than one history of the press cites Zang's (considerable) role in that domain. Our focus here lies elsewhere.

This look at a nineteenth century Austrian entrepreneur was born from efforts to answer a simple question: W*ho brought the croissant to France?*

It was not, despite a persistent tale, Marie-Antoinette, anymore than it was Austrian bakers who invented the roll during the siege of Vienna (see "Croissant Myths"). The fact that neither story is true might also appear to disprove the croissant's Austrian origins. However, it now appears certain that the croissant was indeed based on an Austrian predecessor—the *kipfel* —and brought to Paris by an Austrian—albeit an artillery officer, not a queen.

And so, to discuss the history of the croissant, one must first look at the *kipfel*.

The Kipfel

In Austria, the pointed little loaves of white bread are called '*Kipfel*,' i.e., 'headkins'.

Curtius, *Principles of Greek Etymology*[1]

BEFORE THE CROISSANT, there was the *kipfel*:

"Kipfel" is only one name given to this crescent-shaped pastry, and itself sometimes appears as *kipferl* or *kipfl*. A more archaic spelling is *chipfel* (also subject to variations). Almost as common is *gipfel*, which literally means "peak" or "pinnacle": "The *Gipfel*, or pinnacle cake, which has the form of a crescent, and contains milk and lard."[2] The word *hörnchen* (literally "little horn"), which also means "squirrel", is used for croissant.

The last term highlights the fact that a crescent-shaped roll can be viewed as resembling not only a crescent moon but a pair of horns. Since both have ancient associations, it is likely that such rolls were produced in the distant past. One French nineteenth century writer on the croissant traces its form back to the Greeks, who supposedly made a pastry in the shape of a whole bull: "The Pythagoreans constructed cakes in a bovine shape, which were made with flour and honey." Such cakes, he writes, were used to replace bloody sacrifices of the real thing. associating it with "the Polar Cow" (said to be an ancient name for the Big Dipper) and only over time had this been reduced to a pair of horns, which were then baked as *Selenes*, crescent-shaped pastries dedicated to the moon goddess.[3]

The item ends with this bit of philosophy: "Our croissants, first sacred cake, are now only bourgeois bread, after the religious use, use period, then banal vulgarity, this is the constant rule in matters of human invention."

An official report from 1869 by (strangely) a monuments commission provides a long entry on the kipfel, listing similar pastries referenced in antiquity.

> People all over the world associated any such pastry with the self-renewing, sickle-shaped moon. For the Greeks sickle-shaped pastry was very common and called Episelenion. Apollo, Artemis, Hecate and the moon were given horned cakes as propitiatory offerings. Moon cake is also mentioned in the Bible, as in Jeremiah vii.18: "The women knead their dough, to make cakes to the queen of heaven. [*In the German, the reference is specifically to Melecheth, the Moon Goddess.*]"[4]

The report even explores the pastry's symbolic associations:

> Jupiter Ammon has ram's horns, Bacchus, Silenus, Pan and Satyrs have horns, Alexander the Great did when he was already deified in his life time..., as we see Osiris' and Moses' horns. All these indicate horns referred to the sun or at least to the sunbeam, and as the full horn of the goat Amalthea (the Nourishing) showed the maturing power of the sun's rays, it was also the drinking horns of Ur among the Germans as a symbol of the power of light; of healing ourselves. ... the Kipfel is also a rolled up triangular sheet of dough and everyone knows that the Trigon... retains a certain significance... as a sign of the blessed Trinity.

Much of the above is speculative. But crescent rolls are documented early in the Christian era. A list of a convent's "table blessings" from the tenth century includes the phrase "*Panem lunatem faciat*", which is glossed as follows:

> Panis lunatus - Small crescent-shaped rolls of the finest flour were eaten in convents, and especially during fasts. They are still known in various parts of Switzerland under the name of *gipfel*.[5]

Enenchel's rhymed 13th century chronicle records the fact that in 1227, the Viennese bakers gave Duke Leopold the Glorious of Babenberg "*chipfen*" (an early variant of *chipfeln/kipfeln*) for Christmas:

> Dô brâchten im die pecken
> chipfen und weiʒe flecken,
> weiʒer dann ein hermelein.[6]

In 1630, "*Kipfer*" were recorded in the files of the Vienna Medical Faculty. In 1652 a patent was issued for them. (Note that these references are all dated before 1683, a year of some importance in both kipfel and croissant lore.) Abraham a Sancta Clara (1644-1703) wrote of "long, short, curved and straight kipfel".

In 1757, Trieste (then part of Austria) established standards for their fabrication: "*Mundsemel*, and *Kipfel*, are to be made uniquely of the best flour."[7]

As it happens, Italy, at least in the north, had two similar pastries at one point: the *chifele*, whose name seems derived from the Austrian *chipfel*, and the *cornett'* "so called because of its horned or little horned... shape."[8] And so Italy might, but for an historical accident, have given the croissant to France. As it is, in some regions of Italy today, *cornetto* refers to... a croissant.[9]

Though many authors do not even bother to mention the distinction, older tales about the croissant in fact concern the kipfel. In such tellings, the kipfel is essentially treated as being a croissant under another name. This is not unlike discussing the mammoth and calling it an elephant. How many croissants, like the "pinnacle-cake" cited above, contain lard (which is still used for some kipfel today)?[10]

Kipfel also have long been made in a wide variety of ways, often being covered, for instance, in salt, anise seed, caraway, etc.[11] Several recipes for kipfel, like this one from 1906, describe a sweet:

Wiener Kipfel

5 oz. butter.
6 oz. flour.

2 oz. sugar.
2 oz. sweet almonds.

Vanilla flavoring.

Cream the butter, add the grated almonds and then gradually the flour. Knead well and form into little rolls about 1 inch thick. Bend round into the shape of horns and bake on a buttered tin. While still hot, roll in castor sugar.[12]

A German-language recipe from 1897 (for Germans in America) includes powdered sugar, cinnamon and cloves.[13] Rugelach, a sweet nut-filled pastry known to many Americans, is in fact a variety of kipfel.[14]

The food historian Alan Davidson writes that the earliest (c. 1905) recipe he could find for the croissant was "an oriental pastry of pounded almonds and sugar."[15] But might it not, simply, have been a croissant based on one of the sweeter forms of kipfel?

On the other hand, this nineteenth century American recipe is very much like one for a nineteenth century, if not a modern, croissant:

VIENNA CRESCENTS OR KIPFEL

Vienna Roll Dough

Divide the dough into small pieces; roll with a rolling pin ½ inch thick; cut into triangles about 3 inches long, and roll these three-cornered pieces out very thin, still maintaining their shape; roll these thin triangles up tight, beginning at the broad side, until within half

an inch of the point, which wet with water and milk, and complete
the rolling; lay them on greased baking pans, in the form of a
crescent or half moon; wash over with milk; bake in a hot oven.

The "Vienna Roll Dough" is prepared "as for Vienna bread" (in several meticulous steps) from "16 lbs flour, 7 ozs press-yeast, 6 qts water and milk (or milk alone), 2 ozs salt, and 4 lbs butter".[16]

This is only one of several recipes in which the kipfel is made from the same dough as Vienna bread; only the shape changes.

Vienna bread started in France as *pain viennois*, which itself started (as will be seen) as the *kaisersemmel*. The kipfel and the kaisersemmel are the fraternal twins of Viennese baking and are frequently mentioned together, as in this English report on the 1873 Vienna Universal Exposition:

> The ordinary bread for breakfast and dinner is the "simmel", a little
> round, rather hard crusted roll, with the four flaps of the crust
> meeting in the centre of the upper surface....The breads generally
> met with at the cafés (for a basket of bread is always brought with
> the coffee) are sweeter and more of the fancy kind. They consist of
> the "kipfel", a semi-lunar roll, tapering off at the ends, and
> something like, only smaller than, our milk rolls.[17]

Like the croissant and the kipfel, the kaisersemmel has its own myths; but two nineteenth century Austrian sources credibly date it back to the fifteenth century: "*Kaisersemmeln* owe their name to kaiser Frederick IV [(1382–1439)]". A chronicle records that these originally bore his image (the modern shape might be considered suggestive of a crown).[18]

Otherwise, variety aside, "kipfel", even in its plainest, croissant-like form, has probably meant somewhat different things over time. We are unlikely to ever know, for instance, what exact pastry was presented to Duke Leopold in 1227. Simply put, foods evolve. The blancmange, once a meat-based dish made with almonds, is now a jellied sweet. The profiterole, once a bread made to be stuffed, today is a filled pastry.[19] The typical American macaroon is made with coconut, unlike the older European versions, made from almonds.

This is particularly true in baking. The use of yeast in bread is now standard; in seventeenth century France it was new, and controversial. Crusts have been glazed with egg yolk, but also with steam. Even if bakers over the centuries made what they thought to be a traditional pastry, simply incorporating new, once-unknown techniques (such as using yeast) would have produced a significant difference in the final product.

The rare recipes that can be found suggest that early croissants were very much like the plainer form of kipfel, and the very first croissant almost certainly *was* a kipfel. But the reader should bear in mind that, even if they were briefly the same, the kipfel and the croissant long ago went their separate ways.

Croissant Myths

CULINARY HISTORY IS FULL of colorful tales. Even prominent food historians are often happy to repeat some picturesque account of a food's origin without, it seems, doing the most fundamental research to verify it. The two stories examined here are not the only ones told regarding the French croissant, but they are by far the most widely repeated.

The Siege of Vienna

Innumerable writers date the creation of the croissant to the siege of Vienna by the Turks in 1683. One common version of this tale is that Viennese bakers working late at night heard the Turks trying to tunnel into the city, and gave the alarm. They were rewarded by being allowed to make a roll in the shape of the Turkish crescent. This roll, of course, would have been a kipfel, not a croissant, but few writers make that distinction. (Related stories trace the bagel and the kugelhopf to the same siege.)[20]

This tale appears to be an old one in Vienna, though it does not always end with the invention of the kipfel. In his periodical *Household Words*, Charles Dickens describes a similar incident dating from 1627 and mentions a tavern called the Turks' Cellar, whose name derived from this incident, in which the tunneling Turks were supposedly drowned. Nothing is said about a pastry being invented:

> But I know from the testimony of a venerable old lady ... that the baker's apprentices were formerly allowed special privileges in consideration of the service once rendered by some of their body to the state. Indeed the procession of the bakers, on every returning anniversary of the swamping of the Turks, when they marched horse and foot from the Freiung, with banners, emblems, and music, through the heart of the city to the grass-grown camp outside the city walls, was one of the spectacles that made the deepest impression on this chatty old lady in her childhood.[21]

Clearly the tale, with or without kipfel, was a popular one. A novel from 1858 repeats the tale of "the *Gipfel*, or, as the Italians pronounce it, *Chifel*".[22]

Other variations exist, and some even name a specific baker at a specific address:

> The Crescent or Vienna Kipfel originated with baker Peter Windler and his wife, who had a bakery at number 841 Gruenangergasse, Vienna, at the time the Turks beleaguered the city. This baker had that patriotic, humorous idea to give his rolls the shape of the half moon or crescent, the emblem of the Mohammedans. His crescents found a ready sale... In the house above mentioned a bakery has been operated since 1585 up to the present day.[23]

However, says the monument commission's report, this man died in 1680 —three years before the siege.

The tale of the siege of Vienna is repeated by many "authoritative" works, none of whom cite any period sources for it. Yet if the bakers had in fact saved Vienna, the incident would not only be mentioned in culinary histories, but in any extended history of that city. A glance at several of these shows this not to be the case.

Given how widely repeated the story still is today, one might think that questions about it were relatively recent. But in fact it was challenged more than once before the twentieth century.

The 1869 report refers to this account as a "folk tale", before citing the thirteenth century bakers' gift to Duke Leopold. Writing in 1879, Karl Schimmer discussed the Turkish siege and not only pointed out that alerts had already been set up all around the walls of Vienna to detect tunneling, but that the house in which a baker's apprentice supposedly heard the Turk's tunneling "would be about one-third of the extreme breadth of the city" from the wall.

> This incident is in itself highly improbable, I may almost assert impossible. Not to take into account that it is mentioned in none of the narratives of the time, of which I have fourteen before me, the distance alone would make it next to impossible that so long an operation could have been carried on without detection.[24]

Such quibbles—supported though they were by historical references—did little to slow the spread of what is, after all, a good story. Even the venerable *Larousse Gastronomique*—as late as 2001, in a "Completely Revised and Updated" edition—offers this tale with an even more egregious twist, setting it in Budapest in 1686.[25] This variation baldly demonstrates the cavalier attitude with which even serious food historians present colorful tales. In 1686, the Turks were not the besiegers—they were the besieged:

> In the middle of June, 1686, the city of Buda, on the right bank of the Danube, and now united with the city of Pesth on the opposite bank, was attacked by the Imperial forces under the Duke of Lorraine....On September 2 at six in the morning the assault was delivered, and by the close of the day, after fearful slaughter, the city was carried. The fall of Buda proved the death-blow to Turkish rule in Hungary...[26]

It seems almost superfluous then to remind the reader of what has already been demonstrated: the kipfel existed well before 1683, and so any story setting its invention at that time would be suspect from the start.

Marie-Antoinette

The Austrian-born Marie-Antoinette was perhaps France's most elegant and glamorous queen, and the oft-repeated idea that she introduced France's most elegant breakfast food has sufficient poetry to have endured. If, after all, one accepts the idea that Austrian bakers had only a century before invented the ancestor of the croissant, it is but a short step to imagine that this Austrian princess then brought it to France. This passage from 1996 is only one of many to make that leap:

> The baker boys were granted the privilege of creating a rich roll in the shape of a crescent, the Turkish emblem. These rolls were enormously popular with the Viennese, who called them *kipferl*. When Marie Antoinette left Vienna to marry Louis XVI, she missed these tasty treats so much that she sent for an Austrian baker to teach his Paris confrères how to make them. Transplanted as croissants, they became yet another "French" delicacy introduced by a foreign queen.[27]

But this claim only appears well after the eighteenth century, despite the fact that French queens in general, and Marie-Antoinette in particular, were closely watched and chronicled. Had Marie-Antoinette brought any food into fashion the fact would have been widely mentioned in the gossip sheets of the time. Yet the closest thing to a period reference for this tale is a tantalizing note by her maid, Mme. Campan, that the Queen had a particular preference for "a sort of bread she was used to having since her childhood in Vienna". Also, a list from 1780 of those serving the Queen includes a "German" cook (that is, someone from the Holy Roman

Empire of the German Nation, which included Austria). The cook (who was paid 2,250 livres) probably did make kipfel, though the queen's breakfast was more likely to have been a kaisersemmel.[28] Nothing shows however that he "[taught] his Paris confrères how to make them"; Marie-Antoinette's consumption of her native treats appears to have had no wider influence (which is surprising, given the attention paid to every royal move).

Another canard about the queen might be taken as evidence of this. It should no longer be necessary today to point out that Marie-Antoinette did not say, "Let them eat cake." Still rumors claiming she had were real enough. The French version, however, has her saying, "Let them eat *brioche*". Had her name been associated with another fine bread, it is hard to imagine that more than one satirist would not have thought it clever to substitute "croissant" for "brioche".

Otherwise, it is always problematic to demonstrate the absence of a reference, and in this case, all that can be said for the most part is that neither the kipfel nor any baked good closely associated with Marie Antoinette is mentioned in the more common sources on life in that period. However, it can at least be demonstrated with some certainty that neither the kipfel nor the croissant was known as a breakfast food during the Queen's reign.

While breakfast tends to be the least documented meal, especially for the Old Regime, as it happens an exhaustive list of upper-class breakfast foods was printed just years after Marie-Antoinette's execution. In 1799, Mme. Genlis produced a German phrasebook for aristocrats fleeing France. The book provides translations for an exhaustive list of breakfast items, including "Fresh butter, wheat bread. Milk-bread. Black bread. Rye bread....Toasted slices of bread. Buttered bread.....biscuits, cakes, preserves, ... pastries, dry pastries, old bread, fresh bread..." and all manner of meat, cheese, eggs, and fruit.[29] Neither kipfel nor croissant are mentioned.

Also, had anyone at all introduced the croissant before the nineteenth century, that use of the word (which literally means "crescent") would have soon appeared in dictionaries of the time. But the first, scattered references to the croissant as a pastry do not appear in print until over fifty years after the death of France's Austrian-born queen.

Enter, The Croissant

At the mid-point of the nineteenth century, references to the croissant began to appear in France:

> I have found nothing [in London] comparable to our first quality of split white breads, to our so-called coffee rolls, to our fancy rolls called *Viennese, of dextrin, gruau, croissants...*[30] (1850)

> In upscale bakeries they also prepare, and ordinarily in the semi-circular rolled form folded in, drawn at each end, small breads called *croissants...* [31] (1853)

The second reference here is from Payen's *Des substances alimentaires*, where, along with English muffins, croissants were listed as "breads of fantasy and luxury", that is, what the English call "fancy breads". Such breads were out of the ordinary in form and/or composition and tended to be more expensive.

It was some time however before this definition of the word *croissant* appeared in dictionaries. Littré's dictionary defined it in 1863 as "a little crescent-shaped bread or cake".[32] By 1872, the pastry was sufficiently well-known for an Englishman— Charles Dickens—to write of: "the dainty croissant on the boudoir table."[33]

Its popularity was so established by 1897 that one writer said it was time to "save certain rare forms [of bread] from oblivion since the croissant is starting to replace them everywhere," then added, "The *croissant*, so delicious when properly made, only dates from the middle of the current century." [34] That is, again, around 1850.

Given that it once took some years for a word that had come into common usage to make it into printed texts, this raises a question: what happened in the decade or so before 1850 to make the croissant familiar in France?

The answer is: August Zang's *Boulangerie Viennoise*.

August Zang, "Baker"

92, rue Richelieu.

AUGUST ZANG BEGAN HIS ADULT LIFE as an officer and ended it as a wealthy banker and mine-owner. His involvement in the bakery business was brief, a way-station on the road to his *real* success, and possibly even an embarrassment to him in later years. Future generations might have found this ironic, had those most affected not been blissfully unaware of his impact on their daily life.

Christopher-August Zang was born on August 2, 1807, the son of the prominent Viennese surgeon Christophe Bonifacius Zang (1764-1835), for whom "Zang's space" is named. He dropped out of school early (which may have contributed to problems with his father), went into the military and soon became an artillery officer. Having studied technical chemistry, he at one point tested samples for the building industry. He also invented a new infantry rifle.

The romanticizing tendency that seeps into culinary histories has also colored accounts of Zang's life, so that some such histories refer to this son of a surgeon as, variously, "Count", "Baron" and even "Chamberlain". As it happens, the poet Heine's brother was made a baron for efforts in journalism very much like Zang's.[35] But neither that nor other of these titles are mentioned in those German language sources which document Zang's own life, rather than his part in baking history. His father, on the other hand, was an imperial counselor, perhaps giving Zang access to the highest reaches of Vienna society.

His father died on September 10, 1835, and Zang, at 28, inherited enough money to live, for a time, grandly.[36] In an 1888 article on the Vienna press, H. M. Richter writes that Zang then set up a luxurious apartment, kept fine horses and a carriage and frequented, as best he could, the Viennese nobility. But he soon went through most of what apparently had been a substantial fortune, and also realized that fine horses and a carriage were not enough to make a name for himself.

The Boulangerie Viennoise

By one account, Zang was 21 when he went to Paris.[37] If so, however, this would only have been for a visit. An Austrian list of military officers from 1836 still includes him (as a second-lieutenant).[38] He seems to have changed cities in the following year, around the time he turned 30.

What prompted this Austrian officer with some technical skills to leave Vienna and found a bakery in Paris? Some sources claim that French officers visiting Vienna were so impressed by the bread they tasted there that the entrepreneurial Zang saw an opportunity and brought Austrian bakers with him to found his famous "Viennese Bakery" (*Boulangerie Viennoise*):

> Viennese breads were imported, as their name indicates, from the capital of Austria. They appeared in France during the reign of Louis-Philippe. Princes from the royal family of France, being in Vienna, praised the exquisite taste and the lightness of these breads which they had been served at a formal dinner; they added that these Viennese breads would be highly appreciated in Paris. These words did not fall on deaf ears: they were heard by an officer of the Austrian artillery, named Zang, who resigned his post and came, with bakery workers from Vienna, to set up in Paris, on the rue de Richelieu, a Viennese bakery.[39]

While this is not impossible, one is left to wonder how a then-obscure officer found himself in this company and if this, too, is a culinary legend.

Barbaret tells largely the same version, but adds that Zang only hired his workers for a year (which no doubt made it easier for others to hire them away when their bread became popular).[40]

Other sources say, more prosaically, that Zang, having been to Paris, was displeased with the bread there, which he found "bland".[41] If the reader wonders how Zang could have failed to appreciate France's much-admired bread, one answer is that French bread at the time was not the bread many now know. Earlier in the century, an English visitor wrote: "Even the best French bread in Paris, if I may be allowed to decide in a matter of taste, is far inferior to the bread commonly made in London."[42] While others disagreed, he was not alone. The standard French bread was then sourdough bread, like the dense, chewy *pain de campagne* ("country bread") which has only recently returned to favor. The more expensive fancy breads (*pains de luxe* or *pains de fantaisie*) used yeast and sometimes milk, but were inferior to Viennese breads both in the materials and methods used to make them.

It was also a good time to start an upscale business in Paris. France was then under its third monarchy since Napoleon's fall, but it was a monarchy that favored the upper middle class. After two of Louis XVI's brothers—Louis XVIII and Charles X—, their cousin, Louis-Philippe, now sat on the throne. "Louis-Phillipe's primary supporters came from the upper bourgeoisie. Lawyers, financiers, stockbrokers, and substantial farmers now surrounded the king."[43]

Richter writes that Zang then returned to Vienna to study the baking business: not only how to set up a Viennese bakery and how ovens were made and worked, but also how to deal with other business leaders. One thing he did not study: baking itself. "It is often claimed, inaccurately, that Zang learned baking, was even a baker."[44] In later years, many would attach the label to Zang, and not always kindly. But he was hardly more of a baker than Thomas Watson, who built IBM, was a computer programmer. He *was* a sometime inventor who had studied chemistry and would later obtain a patent for "bread-making methods". So it is possible that at some point he, as the French say, "put his hand to the dough". But his true talents were very modern ones: identifying, developing and managing new businesses and business models.

While back home, he also married his first wife, Marie Wasshuber, whom Richter describes as "a young, beautiful girl from a good family" and (not incidentally) "equipped with a substantial dowry". In August of 1838, he gave up his home in Vienna and resigned his commission.[45]

Initially, Zang had a fellow officer as a partner. After recruiting bakery workers in Vienna, Ernest Schwarzer, a noble from Heldenstamm, followed Zang to Paris in 1837, and helped found the famous bakery. One source refers to "Zang & Schwarzer's pain viennois".[46] But he left the following year to work with a brewer in England, after which he went on to Hungary to work in agriculture, Prague to publish statistics, Moravia to manage forges, and Trieste to direct a newspaper and also help route a postal coach from India through the area; all this before reappearing in Vienna in 1848, where he edited several papers and served in both the legislature and the cabinet.

He was, in a word, as industrious a man as Zang, and perhaps more restless.[47] Did the partnership end because they were too much alike? At any rate, Zang soon had the business to himself, and Schwarzer goes unmentioned in most accounts of it, though in 1848 Emile de Girardin's *La Presse* referred to him as "the same man who founded the Viennese bakery in Paris."[48]

If the two officers came to Paris in 1837, it would have taken some time to establish the business, which finally opened in... 1838? Or 1839? Accounts differ. Writing on the gourmet Brillat-Savarin, Giles MacDonogh says:

> In 1838, only a dozen years after Brillat's death, the Austrian August Zang (1807-1888) moved in at number 92 rue de Richelieu—a few doors up from Brillat's flat at number 66—and opened the Viennese baker's shop that would coin the word 'viennoiserie'.[49]

Barbaret and Kerohant give the same date. But in late 1839, a note in *La Presse* stated: "We see a Viennese bakery being formed under the auspices and direction of a former Austrian officer, M. de Zang," which might suggest it was just being opened.[50] (Note the aristocratic "de"—was it Zang himself who let it be thought that he was a noble? The particle at any rate disappeared in subsequent mentions.) It was only towards the end of this year that the paper began to mention the bakery (and then with some frequency). One Austrian writer also gives the date of 1839.[51] It may be that the bakery had technically opened in 1838, but only became a going concern in 1839—some writers say it was slow to find a French clientèle.

The address, at least, is certain: decades later "rue de Richelieu, 92" was enough of a reference for an engraving from the 1870's, showing two elegant women and a red plush divan, to be entitled, simply, "Le Bon Ton, Paris rue de Richelieu, 92."[52] By then, the bakery itself had made the address famous. But when Zang first arrived, the location had its own cachet.

The rue de Richelieu today can gently be described as "undistinguished". Tourists coming from the Palais Royal or the rue St. Honoré may stop at the statue of Molière a short way up the street before continuing on to the Boulevard des Italiens or perhaps to the lovely

Galerie Vivienne. But the street itself, with its scattered coin dealers, anonymous buildings and neighborhood shops is unlikely to hold their attention. Even Parisians would be surprised to learn it was once a fashionable destination.

The Rue de Richelieu in 1851
Facing the Rue St. Marc and Nos. 91 and 96. The corner of No. 94 is visible at right, but the bakery is just out of sight.

Already in 1815, an English general, "visiting" the city after Waterloo, wrote:

> There is something very picturesque and interesting, I think, in the immense long perspective between the tall houses of such streets as the Rue de Richelieu, into which I was led by the Rue Neuve des Petits Champs. This is the Bond Street of Paris, and is a most amusing one. Here every thing savored of the fashionable world. Shops of a more respectable description richly decorated; goods of the most costly kind arranged for display with a very superior degree of taste and even elegance. Numerous equipages with liveried attendants driving about or waiting at the doors. Numberless loungers sauntering up and down, or philandering in the shops, a striking feature among these the foreign officers, particularly

English, all indicating the Rue de Richelieu as the focus of fashionable resort.

The general at that point had his qualms. He found the buildings "worn and shabby", the street narrow and gloomy. What is more, he wrote, like most of Paris, it smelled: "Not all the fragrant odours issuing from that *magasin* of odours, the Cloche d'Or, and fifty others, were sufficient to overpower this most unsavory of smells."

Perfumer on the Rue de Richelieu
(Early nineteenth century)

As will many tourists today, he hurried on to:

> A broad avenue crossing one end of it, and along which flowed a dense and continuous stream of passengers and carriages. I directed my horse's head thither, and in a few minutes found myself in the Boulevard des Italiens. The excitement and interest of that moment will not soon be forgotten. The breadth of the street, the mixture of trees and houses, the number and variety of the immense multitude moving on, all contributed for a moment to electrify me.[53]

Many of Paris' boulevards, however, had not yet been built and so the smaller *rue* had less competition. A few years later, another Englishman also admired the street, even if he quibbled with the characterization of it:

> The *Rue de Richelieu* is called the Bond-Street of Paris. Parallel with it, is the *Rue Vivienne*. They are both pleasant streets; especially the former, which is much longer, and is rendered more striking by containing some of the finest hotels in Paris. Hosiers, artificial flower makers, clock-makers and jewellers, are the principal tradesmen in the Rue de Richelieu; but it has no similarity with Bond street. The houses are of stone, and generally very lofty—while the

Académie de Musique and the *Bibliothèque du Roi* are public buildings of such consequence and capacity (especially the former) that it is absurd to name the street in which they are situated with our own. [54]

When Zang arrived, the street was at its peak. He had only been there for a few years when a French writer drew this impressionistic picture:

> An all-powerful breath animates and impregnates this road, which has become the Corso of Parisian commerce; an incoherent collection of bourgeois houses and sumptuous townhouses, furnished in all its length by rich shops and gleaming signs, land of Canaan of dressmakers and tailors; one finds helter-skelter there banks, insurance companies and pawnshops. Coaches, barouches, omnibuses, incessantly cross this burning pave-stone; the crowd goes in and out of hotels garnis into cafés, out of cafés into theaters; at one end the boulevard, at the other the Carrousel.[55]

The houses had improved since the general's visit. In 1842, an English writer noted "how richly some of the new houses in and about the Rue de Richelieu are sculptured, so as to present the appearance of a succession of palaces."[56] Two fountains, one with the statue of Molière and the other at the Place Louvois, were built around this time.

Some of the new buildings had been built by the society tailor Buisson. These were a short distance up from the bakery, at 112 (formerly 108), which for so long had been occupied by Frascati's. As it happens, Zang arrived just as a change in the law forced the closing of this famous gambling house, where "the apartments [were] magnificently furnished, and dinners, suppers, and expensive wines [were] given to promote the grand object of such establishments".[57] (Frascati also has a place in food history, since it offered some of the earliest—possibly the first—ice cream cones.[58])

"Women were admitted to *Frascati*; no need to say what kind of women they might be."[59] Looking back in 1875, a writer noted that games of chance could be combined with other amusements:

> No sign for another commerce which nonetheless held sway in the street; one found above shops more than shoes for one's feet, in a world which lived by its receptions. The love affairs rarely lasted beyond a petit-souper. One even gambled there, in the houses of women who had obtained official permission for craps and biribi.[60]

Officially all this ended in 1838. In 1845, William Cullen Bryant wrote approvingly:

> In external morality..., there is some improvement; public gaming-houses no longer exist, and there are fewer of those uncleanly nuisances which offend against the code of what Addison calls the lesser morals.[61]

But unofficially the games went on and the other activities as well.[62]

In fact, wrote Alexander Dumas in 1842, the prostitutes, having been driven (as in the past) from the Palais Royal, were pushed out into the neighboring streets (the rue de Richelieu among them) where:

> The prostitute reappeared under another form, with another dress, and, so to say, another technique.
>
> This depended on that happy Parisian mud it was necessary to confront, and in which it became difficult to drag dresses of cherry velvet, dresses of pink satin and dresses of white *pou-de-soie*, which had done the honor of the [Palais Royal's] wooden galleries.
>
> Further, the streetwalker, who until then had the free use of her two hands, was forced to use one to lift her dress and the other to hold her shawl. It is true that she did not lose all; she no longer showed her bust, but she displayed her leg.
>
> This gave her the false air of an honest woman...
>
> In fact, were it not for that provocative glance, certain movements of the haunches and that continual watchfulness making her look behind more often than before her, the prostitute, thanks to her new outfit, could still fool some freshly arrived rube, who would take her for a lost countess...[63]

Some of the local beauties worked in less scandalous professions. The critic Jules Janin goes on at some length about the street's *soubrettes* (that is, serving-maids, though the word has connotations of "schemer" and more):

> These are for the most part (I speak of the *soubrettes* of the rue de Richelieu) young and pretty women, with white skin, pink cheeks, a fine bust, a provocative glance, a well-turned ankle. There is a whole future of three years of love in these young and pretty slaves of Parisian coquetry. ... They all have the same floating dress, the same white and fine stocking, the same kerchief full of whimsy, and around their pretty head the same Indian scarf, coquettishly and agreeably arranged, turned about, twisted, so well that nothing is more attractive and full of graces than this small mischievous head enclosed in this silk speckled with a thousand colors.

This too, he suggests, was a road to wealth and position:

> These are the aristocrats of the antechamber; they are very near to becoming great ladies and to having servants in their turn. These sorts of fortunes are not rare in Paris. Beauty, youth, freshness, this indescribable quality called by a very pretty French word, *la gentillesse* [kindness, sweetness, etc.], work such changes everyday.[64]

Not that all the women there sought male attention. In 1821 at least, some had taken special pains to *avoid* it:

> Masquerading in men's clothes is not at all uncommon in Paris. I have sometimes seen two or three women at a time dining at the restaurants in this way. No notice is taken of it, and the lady is perfectly safe from insult, though every one that passes may penetrate the disguise... The tailors tell me it is quite a branch of trade—making suits for ladies of a similar taste. There is one particularly, in the *Rue Richelieu*, who is famed for his nice fits to the female figure.[65]

It is not clear if this continued almost twenty years later nor, if it did, if such tailors included fashionable purveyors like Buisson.

Balzac, one of Buisson's clients, later rented a room from the tailor. In 1857, he sang his own praises of the neighborhood:

> Buisson and Janisset, the café Cardinal and the Petite Jeannette (how many breakfasts, deals, jewels, fortunes, in so few words!) form the head of the rue Richelieu. ...
>
> What attraction, what heady sparkling atmosphere between the rue Taitbout and the rue Richelieu....
>
> Once you have put your foot there, your day is lost if you are a thinking man. It is a golden dream and an irresistible distraction. One is at the same time alone and in company. The engravings of the print sellers, the day's shows, the treats at the cafés, the brilliants of the jewelers, all this makes you drunk and over-excites you. All of Paris' upscale and fine merchandise is there: jewels, cloths, engravings, books... One leaves the battlefield of the Stock Market to go to the restaurants, passing from one digestion to another... One thinks oneself rich, in fact one can think oneself clever by continually brushing up against people of wit. So many carriages roll by there that, at moments, one no longer believes oneself on foot. This dizzying movement overcomes you; it is dangerous to stay there, without a chat or an interesting thought.[66]

Though Balzac does not mention Zang's establishment, it would be surprising if he did not at least visit it, not only because of its subsequent fame, but because both men knew the newspaper publisher Emile de

Girardin and Delphine Gay Girardin, his poet-journalist wife. At the least, it is almost certain that they met.

Balzac is the only one of these writers to touch, however briefly, on another advantage of the street: it was near the *Bourse* (the Paris stock exchange), with its associated financiers and related businesses.

At the same time, the street was steeped in culture. The phrase "the rue de Richelieu" was often used as shorthand for the *Comédie-Française* or, less often, for the National Library at the street's opposite end. It was no doubt the Music Academy which drew several music publishers, including, right near the bakery, Maurice Schlesinger (No. 97), whose shop was a meeting place for musicians. One was Wagner, who first met Berlioz there in 1839.[67]

One can readily imagine, then, Zang's potential clientèle: writers, composers, well-off tourists, fashionable ladies out to shop, financiers of every stripe and beauties of uncertain status (be they actress, coquette or soubrette).

Among the street's elegant locales, No. 92 had its own history.

The Hotel de Caumont on the Plan Turgot
(Near the corner of the Rue Saint-Marc)

In 1825, Jean-Jacques Staub, a famous Swiss tailor, bought what was still known as the Hôtel de Caumont. It was named for Armand de Caumont, the Duke de Force, who occupied it in the eighteenth century. In 1778, his grandchildren sold it to a treasurer-general; which is to say, a very rich man. It then passed through other hands before Staub bought it and "entirely rebuilt it"—presumably, like Staub's own creations, in the most up-to-date Parisian style.[68]

To be "dressed by Staub" was then a sure sign of status. In *The Red and Black*—which Stendhal wrote while living on the street (No. 71)— Charles de Beauvoisis is "happy with the cut of Julien's black suit, 'It's from Staub, that's clear'."[69] In *Lost Illusions*, Balzac has Lucien de Rubempré dressed by the tailor: "The next day, towards noon, his first piece of business was to visit Staub, the most famous tailor of this time....Staub went so far as to promise him a delicious riding-coat, a vest and a pair of pants..." When he died in 1852, Staub left a fortune of 300,000 francs.[70] His proximity could only have helped Zang's new business. It may have helped too that he was Swiss (Balzac and others called him "German"; "Germany" at this point referred to the German Confederation, which, among other states, included most of both Prussia and Austria, though not Switzerland).

The address even came with its own colorful—in this case bloody—tale. Just a few years before, in 1835, a tapestry worker had lured a woman to the building's rear courtyard on the pretext of an offer of marriage, robbed and killed her, then cut her up into pieces, a crime for which he was guillotined the following year.

As it happened, the space had recently housed another famous bakery: "Moulet, maker of crusts, easily digested biscuits, and all sorts of pastries."[71] Moulet (or Moullet)'s *croûtes*—"Crusts of Marseilles, Provençal pastry"—were briefly a sensation and are even mentioned in a play from 1833:

> ...already Marseilles unseats
> the little pâtés of Félix.
> Crusts deserve preference,
> Not a gourmet will say no.

A note to this says:

> The *Provençal Pastries* of monsieur Moullet, rue de Richelieu, No. 92, have a fame which cannot escape an honorable mention.
>
> The Crusts of Marseilles, so known in the South of France, are becoming naturalized in Paris, where they are in fashion.[72]

As a confection, "crusts" has meant different things in France. Moullet's were hard enough, like biscuits or bread sticks, to have been taken by sailors to sea, yet fine enough to become fashionable.[73] They were also, it was claimed, excellent for the health:

> Considered from a hygienic point of view crusts possess nutritional qualities not found at all in other pastry products; because apart from their exquisite taste and the fragrance they give off, they can be digested by all stomachs.

> Convalescents speed their recovery if they use them for food;
> children can do without milk if they are given these in porridge; old
> men lacking teeth, feed themselves with them; because this biscuit
> dissolves and does not require trituration; finally, it is a healthy,
> light, comforting and agreeable food. These crusts have the property
> of keeping several years without losing any of their initial quality.[74]

A critic, writing of hack writers, said that some paid for a writer's name as "Moulet, *marchand de croûtes*, paid for his shop's sign on the rue Richelieu."[75] As it happens, this is the second of two articles which criticize the cheap, popularizing publications then becoming common, notably one from Girardin. Fifteen years later, it might have been written about Zang himself.

The bakery's Parisian success was brief; most mentions of it appeared in 1834. Isidore Moullet also had a shop in Marseilles and presumably returned to that city soon after.

Note the reference above to the *Pâtisserie Félix*. This was one of the main draws of the Passage des Panoramas, right nearby, and would outlast Moullet's. An 1855 guide to Paris says "Its cakes *au café*, its madeleines, its babas, its brioches, etc. could not be more appreciated by connoisseurs and gourmets."[76] Though it would ultimately have nothing like the influence of Zang's establishment, Félix stayed foremost for some time.

The gourmet Brillat-Savarin praised another bakery:

> M. Limet, rue de Richelieu: he is the baker of HRH the duke
> d'Orléans and of the prince de Condé; I have adopted him because
> he is my neighbor, and I keep him because I have proclaimed him
> the first bread-maker of the world....
>
> His regulated breads are very handsome; and it is difficult to unite in
> luxury breads so much whiteness, flavor and lightness.[77]

Brillat also praised his neighbor's readiness to experiment. Limet at one point produced a product that might have done well in America, but only had a brief success in France: rolls made with corn meal.[78]

Perhaps a writer had Limet in mind when referring in 1837 to "a bread as glazed and appetizing as if it came from a bakery on the rue Richelieu."[79]

A play from 1853 offers a description (probably simplified and very generic) of a "Pastry shop, rue de Richelieu". This may be based on Zang's bakery, but seems more likely to be of a regular French establishment:

> A boutique — French doors — Entering, on both sides, a counter —
> One, that on the right, loaded with cakes and pastries of all sorts —

That on the left, with breads and a scale: the weights are next to it.
— In the back, a heater on which is a stove surrounded by plates of food. — Two doors, one at left, leading to the furnace; the other opens onto a small very low room. — At right, in the small room, two tables; at left, an enclosed round table. — Then two other tables. — And at the back a door leading to the kitchen.[80]

Clearly, the area's bakeries had a reputation and Zang had competition. Further, by some accounts the French were slow to warm to Viennese baked goods, so that Zang's business was dependent on expatriate "Germans" (Austrians, Prussians, etc.), yearning for familiar products.[81] It could not have hurt that some of these worked for the Rothschild Bank, which sent a wagon to the bakery each day. Says MacDonogh: "The business was slow to take off, but after a certain time his *Kipferl* ('Kiffes' in French) began to sell—literally—like hot cakes, and the croissant was born." [82]

On November 12, 1839, this item appeared in *La Presse*:

> The Parisian public which knows how to appreciate good things goes in crowds to the Viennese bakery and pastry shop, on the rue Richelieu, 92. The elegance of the stores and above all the exquisite merchandise offered there will assure the prosperity of this establishment.[83]

(Like several other mentions in *La Presse*, this appeared, not with the ads on the last page, but interspersed with other news items. Still, given Emile de Girardin's business methods and Zang's own later approach, such mentions were almost certainly paid.)

When Berlioz' *Roméo et Juliette* premiered later that month, Delphine Gay Girardin "did Berlioz the inestimable service of presenting the new symphony as a subject of chat."[84] Simultaneously, she did the same for Zang:

> In truth, what is most discussed after Berlioz's concert is the Viennese bakery which draws crowds on the rue de Richelieu. These exquisite and crisp rolls, framed by superb curtains, lit by brilliant candelabras, make a very agreeable picture for the eye. This new way of composing music and making rolls is quite an event in Paris.[85]

In November, too, Saint-Beuve wrote to a friend: "We are all to go eat some cake Tuesday at a very splendid and very delectable Viennese bakery."[86] (There was, at that point, only one.)

Even on the elegant rue de Richelieu, the bakery stood out for its decor. An 1855 guidebook says "Baking must be a good trade, to judge by the luxury of the shops; some, such as the *Viennese bakery*, on the rue Richelieu, are really splendid."[87] In later years, Viennese bakeries would have a profound influence on the look of Parisian bakeries in general (see "Upgrades and Elegance").

Note that the rolls mentioned above may have been *kipfeln*, but they might also have been the other major Viennese specialty, *kaisersemmeln*. In France, the first became croissants and the second *pains viennois* (Vienna breads or loaves). While the former are far more known today, in nineteenth century France the pain viennois was mentioned at least as often as, if not more than, the croissant. Some credit it with a far more profound effect on French baking (see "The Baguette").

While these two products are the Viennese baked goods most often mentioned, a Viennese bakery would have sold a wide range of other specialties as well, notably *wecken* (hard rolls) and... pretzels. If the idea of eating a croissant-like roll together with a pretzel seems surprising, bear in mind that some types of kipfel were dipped in salt and, conversely, some types of pretzel were made with cinnamon (and in shape were "oblong and tapering, with wavy diagonal lines on the upper side"). Austrian sources of the time include them in lists of "fine baked goods".[88] In the event, however, neither the pretzel nor any other Viennese products left so deep a mark on French culture as the first two.

Austrians also had a sweet tooth, as an English writer noted in 1874:

> The variety of fancy cakes and macaroons is enormous, the chief favourites being chocolate maroons.., "Mandel Kolatchen" (almond knobs) and almond rings. "Patienz Gebacken" (patience pastry) is the nearest approximation to biscuits, being very hard....
>
> "Leb-kuchen" (gingerbread) is another favorite article of pastry... The great objection to this toothsome sweetmeat is that it is far too rich to be wholesome, although this is a recommendation rather than otherwise to the Viennese, who are a confectionery-loving race.[89]

The French however had their own gingerbread and other sweets as well, so if Zang sold any of these, they too left no mark on French baking.

The bakery's popularity with the French did not prevent it from catering to its "German" clientèle. At the end of that same year, this item appeared:

> It is not without pleasure that Germans living in Paris will visit the Viennese Pastry Shop as the New Year draws near. This establishment which has not failed to enjoy success since it opened,

has taken it to heart to give them a souvenir of home in offering them the CHRISTBAUM, decorated with these thousand little things, so desired by all children. This time, it will be Germany which will impose a fashion on France.[90]

Some nineteenth century French bakeries had a special privilege which Zang's may have shared: they could stay open until two in the morning. Already in 1821, Willis, visiting the Passage des Panoramas towards that hour, found Felix "the only shop open from one extremity to the other."[91] In 1852, the poet Gérard de Nerval described going about late at night and looking for a place to eat. One possibility was "the *Boulangerie*, which others call the *boulange*, on the rue Richelieu." But all that was to be found there were "pâtés, sandwiches,— maybe a fowl or a few plates with different cakes, invariably washed down with Madeira."[92]

Was the *boulange* Zang's bakery? Though that is likely—it was the most famous on the street—, one can only guess.

Zang did not neglect his relationship with the French business community. By 1840, he had already joined the Society for the Encouragement of National Industry.[93] Still, relations with his own colleagues were soon strained. Within a decade, the bakery's success had had a noticeable impact on Zang's competitors. In 1845, by one account, the latter went so far as to regularly send chimney sweeps into the bakery to "shop" boisterously at its busiest time. "The maids' pretty white aprons and the fine ladies' clothes suffered from the soot," but the police had no reason to intervene. Ever a practical man, Zang paid the new "customers" off, and the problem was solved.[94]

The bakery's reputation quickly spread beyond France. Already in 1840, a Viennese trade publication said that it had met with "universal acclaim."[95] In 1847, a writer in *Chamber's Edinburgh Journal,* praising changes in French baked goods, wrote that: "the succulent products of the Boulangerie Viennoise are the subjects of general desire and eulogium."[96] These products now included French as well as Viennese specialties. Some were standard; in 1846, Zang advertised for *commis placiers* to go out and sell *biscuits de Reims* (a light sugary biscuit still sold today).[97] At least one was more surprising; in 1858, the bakery offered *profiteroles*, eighteenth-century breads for soup that were already a rarity and, as one newspaper put it, "an inheritance from the old cuisine."[98] At some point, the bakery even began to sell ordinary French bread.

Years after Zang left Paris, the Boulangerie was still a reference: "This same M. Zank [*sic*] ...founded around 1830 [*sic*], in Paris, the famous Boulangerie viennoise"[99]; "[It] seemed to us as fine as if it came out of the boulangerie viennoise of the rue de Richelieu."[100] In 1874, the poet Théodore de Banville gloated that whole volumes of poetry were sold without a single ad while "the Boulangerie viennoise, to sell its bread, ...[is forced] to sink enormous funds into the abyss of advertising."[101]

While most such references no more than mention the bakery, an anecdote from 1852 is set inside it. One morning, a man on the rue de Richelieu scared a huge cat, which took refuge in the bakery:

> Seeing the visitor with its hairs erect, its eye inflamed, pitifully meowing, the young women at the counter were stricken with fear. Their piercing cries only increased the panic of the poor beast which, seeing no exit, threw itself on the counters, overturning and breaking with a great fracas the pastry-filled porcelain, and ravaging, in its aimless bounds, babas, puddings and tartlets.[102]

Lovers of farce may regret that the bakery had just opened, and so was not yet filled with the fashionable ladies in fine dresses who might so deliciously have added to this scene.

Innovations

LA MAIN DE L'HOMME N'Y A PAS TOUCHÉ.
Pain nouveau. **BOULANGERIE VIENNOISE,** Pétri, Moulé
Forme nouvelle. par la machine.
Procédé Rue Richelieu, n° 92, Cuit
purement mé- à la vapeur.
canique. ZANG, breveté du Roi.
DE 6 H. DU MATIN A 6 H. DU SOIR, NOUVELLE FOURNÉE TOUTES LES 1|2 HEURES.
Le Pain en forme de briquettes porte en relief la marque ZANG.

Zang himself may not have noticed the innovation which inspired this book. Viennese bakeries made kipfel as a matter of course and probably neither he nor his imitators saw anything unusual about giving the French "knock-off" a name based on its crescent shape. By the time printed mentions of the French version began to appear, Zang, as we shall see, had other things on his mind. But he was certainly aware that his methods were new in Paris.

In 1842—that is, five years after his arrival in Paris—, he obtained a patent:

31° M. Zang (Christophe-Auguste), baker, living at rue Richelieu, 92, to whom was granted, last April 5th, a fifteen year patent for the invention and perfection of bread making methods.[103]

Two years later, he got a five year extension to this patent.[104]

The unspecified "bread-making methods" probably involved either a mechanical kneader (see below) or Zang's steam oven, which would have such an important influence on modern French bread-making. Though he did not invent this type of oven, one writer says he built his own.[105] It seems certain that this was the first in Paris; by the end of the century, they were standard. Certainly, steam baking was one technique that made his products so unique in France. In that same year, Payen, who would only later mention the croissant itself, described the Viennese method:

> For some time, in Paris, bread has been sold that is called *steam cooked*. Let us explain what is meant by that.
>
> It had long been noticed, in Vienna, that in cleaning the floor of the oven with a plug of moist hay, the batch was finer and the crust of the bread more glazed. It was thought correctly that this result must be attributed to the steam which, in condensing, fell on the loaves. Since then, the floor of the oven was tilted by about 30 centimeters to a meter, the vault being lowered in the front part, and once the item was in the oven, the opening of the oven kept closed with a pad of moist hay; this arrangement allows the steam to fall on the loaves and to obtain a glazed and shiny crust as if it had been first covered with a solution of egg yolk. This is what makes up the steam cooking of so-called Viennese breads, found at M. Zang's, baker, rue Richelieu.[106]

He later gave a revised account of this process, specifying the use of fine flour and milk and crediting the glazed crust to caramelization:

> So-called Viennese rolls are prepared with very white flour, replacing the water used while kneading with a mix of one part milk to four parts water. The crust of these rolls is glazed if the cooking is done in a steam atmosphere. For this purpose, a pad of moist hay is placed on the floor of the oven, cleaned beforehand, producing a cloud of steam. This steam is carefully maintained by the same method, promoting a surface caramelization and giving a very shiny appearance to the crust.[107]

Or as a late nineteenth century English writer explained:

> The glaze upon Vienna bread is the same, and produced in much the same way, as the glaze upon cracknel biscuits... The boiling water in both cases acts upon the surface of the dough, and converts the

starchy matter of the flour into a gummy substance called "dextrine", which is the gum or mucilage of commerce, and is produced by the action of heat upon starch. The starch is first gelatinized by the steam, and then by heat set in a hard glaze.[108]

The French soon refined this method. In 1850, Loriot received a medal for "an apparatus intended to introduce steam into bakers' ovens."[109] At the 1855 Paris Universal Exposition, Jomeau won a medal for "Viennese bakery ovens with a cast-iron shoe to maintain steam."[110] By 1868, this type of oven had already begun to play a central role in French baking:

> It is from Austrian baking that French baking has borrowed, for many years now, the oven called Viennese, which differs from the ordinary oven, notably by a smaller opening and by the tilt of the sole. These arrangements are intended to favor the action of the vapor which comes off the bread while cooking, and which greatly contributes to giving the crust an agreeable color. One progress of French baking, in a decade, consists in the more general use of the Viennese oven, which has been perfected and which several bakers use for ordinary bread; since some time a mixed oven has been conceived, which shares with the Viennese oven a slight inclination of the sole, and which, in several other ways, resembles the normal oven.[111]

One of the most successful of these was designed by Biabaud:

> In the masonry on each side and at the height of the sole, M. Biabaud introduces two recipients in cast iron, which directly receive the heat through two longitudinal cavities. These two recipients are crossed by a lance pierced with holes allowing the steam and the water from a cylindrical boiler... to pass through....
>
> At the right moment, small faucets are turned connecting the lateral recipients with the boiler, and the steam arrives inside the oven, where it acts on the bread to make it spongy, keeps its crust extremely fine, and gives it a fine glazed color.
>
> This system, invented at the end of 1877, was tested by the trustees and the delegates of Paris baking, who found it, apparently, quite superior to everything which has been employed for this purpose until now.[112]

In just a few decades, the technology had moved well beyond "a plug of moist hay".

Some modern sites also claim that the bakery introduced the use of yeast in French baked goods.[113] However, it would be more accurate to say that Viennese methods helped promote its more general use.

Brewer's yeast had been used in bread in France since the seventeenth century—though not without controversy. At least one of Louis XIV's doctors lamented the king's taste for it: "He allowed the king to eat the worst bread in the world, full of yeast and milk."[114]

An eighteenth century encyclopedia resumed the history of its use:

> Normal leavening not having enough strength to ferment the dough of these light & refined breads known in Paris by various names, & which are made with milk, butter & cream, is what obliged recourse to brewer's yeast; but the doctors of the faculty having decided in 1668 that it could be harmful to health, when of bad quality, it was forbidden to bakers, by an act of parlement, of March 20, 1670, to use any but what was made in the city, & which would be fresh & uncorrupted. Experience having shown since that all brewer's yeast is equally good for use in baking, this decision is no longer in effect.[115]

Yeast was soon widely used, if only for fancy breads. In 1856, an English periodical listed some of the breads that had used yeast (but by then were being displaced by new English and Viennese breads):

> The Parisian is so spoilt... that... he will have none but the whitest bread. There are also various fancy-breads, as pain à la reine, pain à la Montoron, pain mollet, pain de Gonesse, pain cornu, pain de Ségovie, in the making of which the yeast of beer, milk, and other ingredients, are used. Many of these are becoming obsolete, or are superseded by pain Anglais... and by pain Viennois.[116]

Raymond Calvel writes: "As may be seen still today on the advertising signs of old bakeries, the consumer had the choice between 'French bread' made from a *levain*, and Vienna-style bread, made from baker's yeast."[117] But this does not imply that the new bread introduced the use of yeast, only that, like the fancy breads before it, the Viennese loaf too was made with yeast. Already in 1836, the "Complete Baker's Manual" discussed the pros and cons of using yeast, either on its own or together with the more traditional sourdough leaven.[118] At this point, it was still mainly used for specialty breads. But by 1871, a later edition of the same work described how the English use of brewer's yeast, in particular, had begun to influence French bread-making:

> In France today, the use of old leavens in making bread is falling more and more into disuse, and, in Paris at least, English style fermentation has greatly spread....

> These new procedures have not only been applied to fancy breads, they have been introduced into the making of ordinary breads as well.[119]

So the question of how yeast was used in nineteenth century bread is complex. Yes, Viennese methods played their part, but other influences (including English bread-making) had also made the practice widespread.

Calvel also says that Zang's Vienna bread "was leavened with a a *poolish*, and was thus a baker's yeast leavened product." One writer goes further: "A Polish nobleman, the Baron Zang, introduced the use of the poolish, a multistage fermentation method based on the use of prepared yeast that is still practiced by specialists today."[120] Zang's Austrian origin aside, no contemporary source mentions his use of a poolish (also known as a "sponge", though some specialists distinguish between these terms).[121] While some Vienna bread was indeed later made using such a pre-ferment, neither Payen nor others who wrote about Zang at the time mentioned this technique. Whether or not he used it himself, it does not seem that Zang introduced the poolish to French bakers.

As it happens, the idea of a sponge had been known (if not necessarily used) in France since at least 1771, when Malouin quoted a memoir he had received from England:

> They make a dough of flour & of water, in which they put enough brewer's yeast to stimulate fermentation; a little salt is added to prevent the yeast from fermenting the dough too much. The dough so prepared is called *the sponge*. The sponge is left in a container for five hours.[122]

If this or any other pre-ferment was used in France in the nineteenth century, it does not seem to have been widely known. In Boutroux's 1898 work on "Bread and Bread-making", he again describes the sponge, as well as two other pre-ferments, as British methods. He mentions nothing similar for French methods.[123] To complicate matters, at least one American writer refers to the old use of a sourdough leaven as a "continued sponge".[124] Such references may have led to the idea that the yeast-based sponge was used in France as well.

Otherwise, confused accounts of sponge and poolish history are beyond our scope here. At the least, whenever or however it came to France, the Polish origin implied in that word is at best uncertain.

Still, if he did not introduce either the poolish or the use of yeast in general, Zang probably used better yeast than French bakers. Decades after he left Paris, the superiority of Viennese yeast was well established :

Everybody was able to see how the Viennese bread was lighter than most French and English breads, this is because in Austrian bakeries pure yeast is used to make the dough. The release of carbonic acid being more uniform, the dough is more homogeneous, thus lighter and better prepared. Besides, thanks to the method of preparation, Vienna yeast cannot contain bitter principals, nor the strong-smelling essential oil contained in hops. These principals dominate, to the contrary, in brewer's yeast and affect all the more bread in which it is necessary to use large doses of this fermenting agent. The quality and the taste of the food gain a great deal from the German yeast; thus many Paris bakers begin to use it and have easily managed to make products as fine and more varied than the Viennese products. Unfortunately, the price of this energetic yeast is too high for it to be used in any breads but those of the finest quality.[125]

Yeast was not the only costly ingredient used by Viennese bakers. In 1902, Emil Braun (translating from his own German) emphasized the importance of Hungarian flour (which was just then starting to become more affordable):

"*Vienna*" is really the *Mecca* of the baking fraternity of Europe, as much so as Paris is the Mecca of the "Chef de Cuisine".

The question comes natural [*sic*] - "*What gives the Vienna bakery products their reputation?*"

First, it is the fine flavor; second, the lightness and sponginess; third, the rich color, and fourth, the freshness, small batches being baked every few hours. A great share of the credit for these points can be traced to the famous Hungarian flour. However, it requires a special skill and more care on [the] part of the baker to bake with the hard, rich Hungarian flour than if the common German flour is used. The fermentation must be studied before an otherwise proficient, experienced German baker can bake a good "Vienna Loaf" or "*Kipfel*" and "*Kaisersemmel.*"...

...The flour alone could not produce the fame for the "Vienna Bakery" without the efforts and skill of the baker himself.[126]

While some of the boulangeries viennoises which sprang up after Zang's success did hire Austrian bakers, early French instructions for the "Vienna Loaf" do not mention (then very expensive) Hungarian flour, and the "Viennese products" of Zang's competitors were probably of very varied quality.

Zang was above all a businessman and two of his innovations were in marketing. In 1842, an ad for his bakery proudly proclaimed:

UNTOUCHED BY HUMAN HANDS

New bread.
New shape.
Purely mechanical process.

Kneaded, Molded
by machine.
Steam-cooked.[127]

As MacDonogh puts it:

> All Zang's Kipferl came out of his newly perfected steam oven emblazoned with the words "la main de l'homme n'y a pas touché".
>
> This was a selling point then. Where it might be technically true of McDonald's burgers today, they are unlikely to tell their customers that their food is machine made... [128]

In other words, the same "hand-made" claim that is now considered a selling point was then considered, if not a defect, at least less desirable than to be "machine made". If this seems like an appeal to a love of novelty for novelty's sake, consider this passage from the French nineteenth century "Dictionary of Conversation":

> It is easy to comprehend that in doing so fatiguing a job, the kneader would be covered with sweat; and as this man, almost nude, lifts the dough, holds it between his arms, presses it against his chest, the sweat mixes with the dough, and bakers have been heard maintaining that the warmth of the body is necessary to develop the working of the dough. A process which would work the dough without it being exposed to contact with the worker's body would offer very favorable conditions in regard to hygiene; this has been accomplished by various mechanical kneaders which have been successively invented, but which bakers have generally rejected on flimsy pretexts. The reproaches against mechanical kneaders were well founded in regard to some of them,.... but tests have... proven that several give excellent results in terms of the quality and the kind of bread. A well-constructed kneader must work the dough better than the hand of man, since the latter divides his dough into seven or eight parts, on each of which he only works for part of the time, while the kneader works on all of it at once.[129]

If Zang's claim was true, he very probably did use such a mechanical kneader, well before they were widely accepted in France. (In 1886, Barbaret was still describing workers' resistance to these machines.[130]) But whatever method he used did not draw the same attention as his steam oven and no description of it survives.

One of Zang's most cited innovations did not directly affect the quality of the bread at all. By early 1840, his products were already popular enough to be imitated by other bakeries. In February, an ad appeared in *La Presse*:

> The owner of the BOULANGERIE VIENNOISE ...warns the public that several Paris bakers having sold bread whose form resembles the VIENNA LOAF, but whose quality is infinitely inferior, which will tend to devalue the products of this establishment, all items which come from its ovens will from now on be marked with the sign (ZANG).[131]

MacDonogh says they were in fact stamped: "Zang—Untouched By Human Hands." As a writer in the *Revue de Paris* pointed out, Zang was not quite the first to do this:

> M. Zang, the Viennese pastry chef of the rue Richelieu...thought to immortalize himself in signing his rolls; [but] a roll has been found in an oven, at Pompeii, which I have seen in the museum of Naples, and which bears the name of its author.[132]

This must be distinguished from another stamp which had already been required in previous centuries—not to protect the baker's brand, but to help officials enforce regulations:

> Bakers were ordered to print on the bread that they make, their initials, & to mark at the same time the weight of each loaf, with as many periods as the bread weighs in pounds, in order to have recourse against the baker in case of a defect....[133]

A similar law had been passed in 1824 and was renewed the same year Zang made his announcement, and so all bakers were obliged to stamp an identifier—though not their name—on their bread. It is not clear if Zang's approach would also have fulfilled this obligation, but certainly it was unusual enough to cause comment, then and later.[134]

Zang's Influence

Zang's idea was popular enough to be copied quickly, and very soon other addresses were cited for a "boulangerie viennoise". But his influence went well beyond inspiring competitors.

Already in 1846, an American visitor to Paris wrote: ""How good after it all... a fresh pain viennois"[135]. In the same year, a French writer described one effect of Zang's initiative:

> Importing Viennese bread to France had two results: the first was to satisfy the palate of the most difficult connoisseurs, and the second was to destroy a deep-rooted prejudice, for many years, among all the French who had never traveled to the other side of the Rhine. It was very generally imagined that Germany was an excessively backwards country in terms of gastronomic pleasures, and you could never have made a pure blooded Parisian believe that anything was eaten in Vienna or Berlin other than sauerkraut and rye bread.
>
> Still German cuisine would perhaps be less appreciated in France than Viennese pastry, and we believe it would probably be less prudent to found a *restaurant viennois*.[136]

Hervé de Kerohant describes the impact on Paris bakers:

> The success of the Viennese bakery led Parisian bakers of rich neighborhoods to also make Viennese luxury breads. In 1840, two years after the creation of the Zang establishment, Paris already contained twelve makers of Viennese bread, employing one hundred workers.
>
> In 1845, the consumption of Viennese bread had grown to such proportions that the number of workers in this specialty had climbed to two hundred and fifty. These workers formed a professional association. Twice a week, they met in a café of the passage des Panoramas to discuss their interests, spread their industry and take care of finding employment. Most of these workers had republican and revolutionary ideas, and, in 1848, the Viennese bread workers enthusiastically welcomed the regime resulting from the February revolution.[137]

Barbaret too mentions the radicalism of these workers, which was communicated to those back home—a development which would ultimately be of some importance to Zang.[138]

"Vienna-style" baked goods, then, had quickly become a staple of French bakeries and have been commonplace in France since, even if *viennoiserie* —the term used for them today—itself seems to date from the twentieth century (*Le Correspondant*'s use of it in 1907 appears to be one of the earliest).[139] As with viennoiserie today, not all of these, over time, were of Viennese origin. In 1878, one writer treated the term as being synonymous with "luxury bread":

> Besides the ordinary production.. there is that of luxury breads, called "Vienna-style", which has a great importance in Parisian baking, and which includes all breads with a glazed crust, breads of gruau flour, breads with butter and with milk, whose forms and dimensions are almost infinitely varied. They are made of gruau

flour mixed with milk with butter sometimes added, and prepared with yeast... These breads are prepared and cooked with the greatest care.[140]

The term "Viennese bakery" itself soon became a generic term, both in standard—"He went a long way to buy a loaf of bread at the best Viennese bakery..."[141]—and legal usage:

> A judgment handed down by the Tribunal of Commerce of the Seine on August 29, 1884 (Chaudet vs. Lucas) decides that the term "Viennese bakery" is in the public domain, that it is an obligatory term, necessary to indicate making bread in the Viennese oven.[142]

Was all this inevitable? Given the excellence of Viennese methods and ingredients would they have come to France, and established themselves as strongly, without Zang?

Perhaps. But the references to his establishment's elegance and its popularity with Paris society make it plain that Zang's Boulangerie Viennoise was something more than a bakery—it almost immediately became a social destination. It was, in modern terms, trendy, and would remain so for years. Just as coffee's being splendidly served by a handsome Turkish ambassador helped further its cause in Paris, Zang's "exquisite and crisp rolls" might have been less remarked had these not been "framed by superb curtains... [and] lit by brilliant candelabras."

For anyone who might have thought that Zang had, as it were, lucked into a good thing, he would soon demonstrate his promotional and entrepreneurial skills in a very different arena. His introduction of transformative concepts into France does not seem to have been a fluke.

Elegance and Upgrades

In 1860, the poet de Pons credited—or perhaps blamed—Zang for another development, saying that his bakery had inspired bakers to make "as many cakes as breads."[143] He was not the only writer to point to the Boulangerie Viennoise as contributing to a development which, if it (arguably) began in the nineteenth century, still continues today.

One example in late twentieth century America would be the number of barbershops which were replaced by—or became—"men's salons" or "coiffeurs". Simply put, ordinary, functional businesses often find it advantageous to add a veneer of elegance which may range from a change of name to a more substantial shift in methods and decor.

Already in 1844, the *Magasin Pittoresque* had noted this change in Paris:

> For a dozen years now there has been a revolution in shops: not only have the exterior and interior decoration begun a development whose end is barely in sight, but further the relations between different Parisian industries have undergone great modifications. There have been encroachments by professions one on the other and for some complete changes.
>
> Bakers have become pastry-makers; grocery stores have enclosed with glass their stores once open to the four winds, and they have invaded the empire of confectioners and chocolateers; food-sellers have united the attributes of pork butchers, of fishmongers, of fruit-sellers; fruit sellers become greengrocers or at least orange-sellers, almost botanists; creameries struggle with ice cream makers and provide refreshments at balls and soirées; cafés are glittering palaces; stationer's shops have raised up stores of fantasy where an infinite variety of fun nothings and adorable *inutilities*, as the merchants say, are sold for a price of gold.
>
> On the other hand, the blackened counters of walnut and the yardstick of white wood have disappeared, driven away by mahogany desks, by inlaid woods and by the metallic and gilded meter: smoky oil lamps have given way to bright gaslights; the tiled windows, which seemed rather intended to repulse than to let in the light of day, are relegated to small provincial towns, while floods of light inundate the merchandise through magnificent sheets of glass; finally gold, velvet, silk, polished steel, sparkling copper and crystal compete for the buyer's eye.

The *Magasin* (ironically, the word means "store") would not be the last to credit the rising middle class for these changes:

> It is the arrival in power of the Parisian bourgeoisie which is apparent on all sides, as much by the individual luxury of merchants as by the work of the city municipality; because if one examines closely all these modifications spontaneously introduced in Parisian industry, one sees that they express the tendency of shopkeepers to each raise themselves above his initial competence, and to introduce into his daily routine the habits of taste, of grace and of exquisite cleanliness.[144]

The article goes on to note at least one conflict which grew out of this mercantile ambition: a quarrel between bakers and pastry-chefs. Without taking a detour into that tale, consider this: is the croissant a bread (a roll) or a pastry? The fact that it has been described as both neatly sums up the potential for dispute.

This tendency to upgrade to elegance may then be considered part of the zeitgeist. But it was particularly apparent in the baking world. In 1887, Fayeux looked back at such changes, equating Viennese bakeries with "luxury bakeries" which sold *pains de luxe*, or fancy breads:

> This innovation revolutionized Parisian baking and this revolution would certainly have been to the advantage of the body, bringing it a new source of profits, if it had been possible to limit the creation of luxury bakeries to rich neighborhoods. Unfortunately this was not so.
>
> Bakeries in middle class neighborhoods imitated the Viennese bakeries. The locales they occupied were too small, their clientèle too modest, to allow them, like their fortunate rivals, to put common bread in a back room and to have, for sales and display, a vast and rich store, glazed with mirrors, lined with mosaics with allegorical paintings on the ceiling and rich ornamentation in the panels. But with a few well-placed mirrors, counters and shelves of white marble, a few gilded strips applied on a base of white lead, black and white tiles, the owners of these bakeries obtained *pseudo-Vienneses*, where fancy bread is displayed on shelves at the front of the shop, while common bread is arranged at the back, held up by copper rods, always, what is more, polished and shiny.
>
> The author of this study is an old Parisian, who still remembers the old bakery, before the transformation. The baker did not then seek out luxurious ways, but populous and well-traveled streets. His shop was defended by a grate, made up of thick bars bulging out towards the public way. Behind this grate, a few loaves were placed to serve as a sign. In the shop, counter and shelves were of wood and of a primitive simplicity. Finally, and it is a memory quite immediate for us, like all childhood memories, in most bakeries was found—it was the fashion—a large cage of iron wire, set well in sight and holding a gray parrot. The simplicity of manners went very well with this modest, but sufficient, installation.
>
> Today, the poorest bakery on the outskirts is installed with a ruinous luxury: it too claims to be Viennese, and since the modesty of its sales do not allow the production of fancy breads, it sometimes buys from specialized producers who come to supply it early in the morning with the few rancid croissants which dry behind the windows. This gilded misery weighs more heavily on the small baker; it does not allow him to sell at a low price, as the neighborhood requires, and leaves him no hope of saving some money and rising in his profession.[145]

This "luxury" did not necessarily extend to the back rooms. Fifteen years earlier, the bakery workers' union had warned the public about the poor hygiene in bakeries in general, adding:

> Appearances are deceiving. All these luxurious bakeries where mirrors, painting, sculpture, bronze, marble and gold are piled on ludicrously in order to captivate the client, are not exempt from this lack of elementary care.[146]

Though the changes he described started with the Viennese bakeries—and so with Zang—, Fayeux blamed the worst of what followed on a very modern villain: the deal maker (*faiseur d'affaires*). His analysis has a particular resonance when read in 2009, so soon after the burst of the mortgage-backed securities "bubble":

> This transformation is above all due to a modern plague which causes great upsets: the deal makers.
>
> When it was established that making fancy bread, added to the usual bread, was a source of profit for the baker of the better neighborhoods, a certain number of speculators bought bakery businesses in second-rate neighborhoods, spruced them up, and added Viennese production, busied themselves in giving these establishments a fictitious and so short-lived prosperity; then they profited from a favorable moment to sell the establishment at a large profit and start again elsewhere. All the bakeries of Paris have passed through this successively.
>
> These businesses, sold for the most part on credit, were paid on notes of hand. These notes, following the sales and re-sales of these same bakeries, were endorsed by a whole series of buyers, and, unpaid at term, protested, renewed, they ended by making up the fiction of credit and debit for an infinity of bankruptcies, which dishonored a commerce where, until then, the greatest respect had been shown for commitments.

Plus ça change....

Still, many tourists today are grateful for the ornate nineteenth century bakeries—real or imitated—whose brass, mirrors and marble can, it seems, also be traced back to August Zang.

The Baguette

To the degree that Zang is known today, it is not only for introducing the croissant to France. In that country, he is far more frequently cited as having introduced the *baguette;* that is, the long loaf known the world over as the typical French bread.

> The origin of the Parisian baguette is uncertain, but the most likely hypothesis is that it came from Vienna! It reached Paris in 1840, in a bakery at 92 rue de Richelieu owned by an Austrian who initiated Parisians into his country's traditions.[147]

However, Zang's claim here is a bit more problematic, since the baguette (the bread) is not mentioned in dictionaries until well into the twentieth century and baguette history overall is far from settled.[148]

In fact the baguette, too, has its myths. The *Economist* cites one:

> The baguette was invented during Napoleon's campaign in Russia, gushes the blurb of one [bakery]. Traditional round loaves took up space needed for extra clothes. Napoleon therefore ordered a new shape of bread to be designed that could be carried down the soldier's trouser-legs.

This story can be dismissed on a number of grounds, not least the difficulty of marching with a stick—of anything—down one's pants leg. More typically, writers offer similar stories for the baguette as for the founding of Zang's bakery:

> The Parisian baguette saw its first birth in the form of the Vienna loaves. In 1837, members of the royal family visiting Vienna discovered there a light, appetizing, flavorful bread, which they said could be very successful in Paris. Count Zang, artillery officer and great chamberlain of the court of Austria, came to Paris the following year and acquired a shop at 92, rue de Richelieu which he converted into a bakery. There he installed a new oven, used the finest flour, produced by Hungarian mills, milk, but without yeast. "Zang" bread was quickly all the rage under the name of the "*pain viennois*".
>
> The baguette proper was born around 1890. New ovens, new bread-making methods, use of direct yeast and design of angled vents on top, this will be the new long bread.[149]

This item gives no source for the 1890 date, which cannot be found elsewhere and is, at any rate, unlikely, given the evidence that the baguette appeared in the twentieth century. Otherwise, it is not the only one to link the baguette with the pain viennois—the Vienna loaf. As Patricia Wells wrote in the *New York Times*:

> Other historians suggest that the baguette evolved from the viennois, the Austrian loaf popular around the turn of the century. The loaf, still found in the majority of boulangeries in France, has the same slender form as the baguette, but is sweetened with sugar and softened with milk.[150]

As mentioned earlier, the pain viennois began as the kaisersemmel. Since it existed well before the baguette and today does indeed have the same "slender form", one might easily assume that it inspired the later bread.

The big fly in this logical ointment is that it assumes the nineteenth century pain viennois was shaped like its modern descendant. But this is at best unproven and in fact unlikely, given that its model was the kaisersemmel. What does a kaisersemmel look like? In a word, exactly like the American bread with the same name (translated into English): the kaiser roll.

Anyone who has had a deli sandwich on this less than refined roll might be surprised to know that the Austrian original was long considered the pinnacle of Austrian bread-stuffs:

KAISER SEMMEL (EMPEROR ROLL).

> This is one of the characteristic and best selling Vienna varieties of bread-stuff. A perfect, fine Kaiser Semmel is really the pride of the Vienna baker. The moulding of these rolls is quite a knack, and out of a hundred bakers you may find ten who can mould a Kaiser Semmel properly. Of course in Vienna every baker must be proficient in making this particular roll. Before he can do this, he is not considered a good baker.[151]

Images of the nineteenth century pain viennois are lacking, but numerous sources refer to it as a *"petit pain"*, that is, a roll, not a *"pain"* (bread or loaf): "The *petite* [sic] *pains Viennois* sold at present are delicious".[152] Even those which do not often make it clear in context that the term refers to a roll: "Viennese loaves - These rolls are prepared..."[153] (It does not help matters that Anglo-phone writers of the period often refer to full-size French breads as "rolls"—a confusion which is generally avoided when the French term is *petit pain* instead of *pain*.)

Payen gives a slightly more precise description: "These breads, elliptical, bear a longitudinal groove and transversal rays obtained by very light incisions in the dough."[154] It is true that, later in the century, the dough used for the Vienna loaf was given a variety of shapes (some forgotten today):

> The Vienna loaf has remained in fashion. It is the one generally served in famous restaurants and in comfortable houses. It is presented in different ways: slender and cracked, in corkscrews, round and with five splits: the latter is called "the Emperor". There is also the little Richelieu mirliton and the brahoura or navette.[155]

Even if the original shape was now known as "the Emperor" (a literal translation of *kaiser*), the other shapes, such as the navette, were also rolls, not full-size loaves.

A rare mention (from 1897) of Vienna bread as a full-size loaf refers to a "Viennese jocko".[156] This would indeed have resembled a baguette. But here it would have been the Vienna bread that was imitating an existing loaf, that is, a *jocko*. The jocko was one of several very long breads—often six feet in length—made in nineteenth century France. Though there is some disagreement about whether it was made from standard dough or the finer dough similar to Viennese dough, it was a distinct type of its own; a full-size jocko, with its slanting *grignes*, looked very much like a giant baguette.

It would be reasonable, in fact, to suggest that the baguette developed from the jocko. But there is no more specific evidence for that then there is for the bread having started as a Vienna loaf. The best that can be said is that the nineteenth century Vienna loaf was not typically like a baguette and very likely did not give rise to it.

When did French bakers begin to shape the Vienna dough like today's baguette? Very probably, after the baguette itself became popular. Raymond Calvel offers one explanation:

> The so-called Vienna breads and rolls that began to make an appearance toward the end of the 1940s partially replaced *farine de gruau*-based baguettes and rolls, since production of these latter products was essentially forbidden from August 1940 to September 1956.[157]

However, since Vienna breads themselves had been made with gruau flour (and long before most French breads), the question arises of why they would have been preferable in this case.

A member of the celebrated Poilâne bread dynasty says that the baguette "was imported from Vienna in the late 19th century".[158] This seems very unlikely, even if Paul Richards wrote in 1918 that "the French bread of today is not at all genuine French; a large part of it is really a Vienna loaf, it is made with the Vienna process, only in the large loaves the milk is left out."[159]. While the influence of Viennese baking on the French is certain (see below), there is no period evidence that anyone from Vienna, much less Zang himself, brought the baguette in particular to France.

The most likely date for the appearance of the baguette is given in an article from the *Economist*, which credits the bread's creation to a change in labor law just after World War I:

> The French word for baker is *boulanger*, he who makes *boules*, or round loaves, not a "*baguettier*" who makes sticks. In fact the baguette dates back to the 1920s, and its progress has done to traditional French baking what the white sliced has done to the British loaf.
>
> Changing technology was partly responsible for the baguette's introduction. By the 1920s most French bakeries were equipped with the steam ovens needed to caramelize the starch on the surface of the loaf to give it a golden, slightly translucent crust. History also played a part. The first world war created a shortage of manpower and traditional loaves prepared from a sourdough became too labour-intensive for many bakers. But the coup de grâce was legal. In October 1920 a new law came into force that prevented bakers from working before 4 am, which meant that they did not have time to bake a fresh *boule* for the breakfast table. They thus turned to the rapidly prepared baguette.
>
> The baguette was a wow. Bakers liked it because it was convenient to make and stayed fresh for only a few hours. Hence customers visited bakeries two or three times a day. Consumers liked the baguette because it is whiter and sweeter than sourdough breads.[160]

Unfortunately, the *Economist's* article is inaccurate on several points, notably the implication that it was the baguette which displaced the *boule*. The jocko and similar long breads had already done that all through the nineteenth century. As for the baguette being "whiter and sweeter"—because made with yeast, rather than leavening—this would not in itself have been a great change. The French had long favored the whitest bread they could find, first rejecting (very healthy) whole wheat (dark) bread and then, increasingly, sour dough bread. In 1856, Husson wrote:

This pronounced taste of the consumer of every class for white, fine bread does not date from yesterday. "It was about thirty years ago", says Delamare, "when this statute was handed down (that of March 30, 1695), that sensuality began to make its way into bread-making."

But it was the Parisians who pushed this luxury in food far. Formerly, they had *pain à la Reine, pain à la Monteron, pain mollet, pain de Gonesse, pain cornu, pain de Ségovie,* all types in which the use of brewer's yeast, milk and other ingredients played the principal role. Today, the nomenclature of fancy breads is somewhat simplified though rolls of a particular composition are still made for certain gourmets, such as English and Viennese loaves, it is above all the white color and the taste which please the Parisian, and these advantages, desirable from the hygienic and nutritional point of view, he readily gets, thanks to perfected milling. One must not then be surprised that the use of dark bread has almost totally disappeared from Paris, and if this sort of bread only appears exceptionally, on the modest tables of small households.

Already under Napoleon, dark bread was losing favor with all classes, as a committee noted in 1812: "'No class wanted to eat [inferior bread], ... one had certain proof in the dark bread which was brought daily to the market and which found few buyers, although the price was very modest."[161] While bread made with yeast and sometimes milk was still a luxury at that time, by 1884 the *New York Times* wrote:

> The genuine Parisian population will not look at brown bread; its bread must be "first category bread;" more still, it is beginning to insist not only upon "first category bread," but to crave for what is called *pain de luxe,* that is, bread made after the Vienna fashion, of the very finest flour. Twenty years ago only half a dozen bakers in the central district offered for sale this bread "*a la Viennoise,*" at present in every quarter every bakery must have its so-called *Viennois* baker or lose its customers; it must offer its *pain riche,* its *pain jocko,* its *pain allemand,* its *pain de gruan* [sic], &c, without counting on an infinite variety of *petits pains.*[162]

And so the baguette was not a revolution in that sense. It is not clear, either, that the bread was a "wow", given that major periodicals like *Le Figaro* and *La Presse* made little or no note of it. Further, the *Figaro*'s first mention of it, in August 4, 1920, precedes the implementation (in October 1920) of the 1919 law, so even that connection may be fortuitous.

Still, the first mentions of the baguette as a bread, both in English and in French, are from the early twenties (it took much longer for that meaning to appear in dictionaries).[163] By all evidence the term (if not necessarily the bread) appeared around that time.

How then does Zang get credit for it?

The answer lies in that steam oven, introduced, with other methods, at the Boulangerie Viennoise. Schirmaker, in 1908, noted the technical influence from the East:, influences which began with Zang: "In a general way, Parisian baking has been reorganized and modernized by German and Viennese bakers (new oven system, use of steam, special flour)."[164] Clearly by 1920, the technical infrastructure was already in place to produce a baguette and probably was incrementally established through the late nineteenth century.

Its implementation, however, certainly began with Zang and his steam oven, and so the food writer Elizabeth David here unknowingly credits Zang with introducing, not just the croissant and the baguette, but, in a word, modern French bread:

> It was the Viennese oven, with its steam injectors and its sloping floor, or sole, which was mainly responsible for creating the tradition of French bread as we know it today. English bakers, and indeed many of the older French ones, still call this type of bread 'Vienna' bread, the true French bread being the old round or cylindrical hand-shaped *"pain de campagne"* or *"pain de menage"*.[165]

The changes David describes are only some of those introduced, as we have seen, by Zang. Already in 1847, a writer in *Chamber's Edinburgh Journal*, speaking of both white and brown bread in eighteenth century Paris, wrote:

> At that period, the Parisians were far behind the rest of Europe in the making of fine bread. At the present moment, however, they have nothing to learn; the bread displayed in the windows of the magnificent *boulangeries* of Paris is of exquisite delicacy.[166]

The writer then goes on (as previously quoted) to praise Zang's bakery in particular.

In 1880, an American paper too gave Zang credit for the improvement in French bread:

> The best bread in Paris now-a-days is but an imitation of the Vienna article, by the introduction of which about thirty years ago a gentleman by the name of August Zang, then the proprietor of the *Boulangerie Viennoise*, rue Richelieu, realized a rapid fortune.[167]

In 1899, a writer in the *Magasin Pittoreseque* summed up the new state of affairs:

When one stops, by chance, a few moments before an elegant Parisian bakery, one feels the appetite agreeably tempted by the golden crust of the *flûtes*, the good odor given off by fresh croissants, and the swollen, very white crumb of the "split" breads; but one hardly gives a glance at the *pain boulot;* as for the round bread with its gray crumb and crust, one regards it with disdain and passes it by.[168]

If in fact then Zang was displeased with French bread as he found it, his solution, however inadvertent, was to help change it, so that the French bread we know today is a bread profoundly influenced by August Zang.

Towards the Modern Croissant

THE FACT THAT THE CROISSANT BECAME COMMONPLACE within a decade after Zang opened a bakery selling kipfel makes it plain that Zang introduced the croissant to France. But it is just as plain that the nineteenth century croissant was not the croissant we know today.

The modern croissant can be succinctly described as a crescent-shaped puff pastry made with yeast (as is not true of all puff pastries). Puff pastry —*pate feuilletée*—had been known in France since the seventeenth century, when it already involved multiple applications of large amounts of butter to the dough.[169] But an 1853 description of the croissant—it is not quite a recipe—mentions neither butter nor puff pastry:

> The liquid used to form the dough with one kilogram of flour is made with one or two eggs beaten and mixed with about five hundred grams of water. Otherwise the choice of the flour, the dose of yeast, as well as the working of the dough, require the same care as with the other luxury breads mentioned above. [170]

One 1886 list of different fancy-breads says that croissants are "kneaded with butter."[171] The reference to butter is in itself unusual; but presumably if puff pastry (which requires far more than kneading) was intended, the writer would simply have referred to pate feuilletée.

Again, two later specifications (from 1895 and 1897, respectively) mention neither butter nor pate feuilletée:

> Croissants, so called because they have a semi-circular form, are prepared by mixing 1 kilogram of flour of the first quality with 500 grams of water, in which the yolk and the white of an egg have been beaten together.[172]

> Preparation of croissants - For 5 kilograms of flour, blend 100 grams of yeast in a liter of cold milk in summer, or warm in winter. Add flour to make a dough that is not too firm. Leave it to rise in a gentle heat for an hour.

Add the rest of the flour, 60 grams of salt, the necessary quantity of milk; work the dough in the usual way and put it in the oven.[173]

Properly baked, these preparations would have yielded pastries with the gleaming caramelized surface that first characterized viennoiserie. But they would not have had the flaky surface found on the best of today's croissants, and in fact on much modern viennoiserie.

An English recipe from the turn of the century is more extensive (and probably more useful to any reader who would like to make a period croissant):

> *Croissants.*—These French rolls are simply made with French, milk, or Vienna dough; or any good household dough will do if made with half milk, half water, with a little butter rubbed up into the dough at the second kneading. About 3 1/2 oz. of butter to the quartern of dough is the right amount. When the dough has risen the second time, roll it out like pastry, about ¼ in. thick, cut it into even squares, and each across diagonally into two triangles; take a corner at the ends of the longest side of the triangle in each hand, with the third point outside away from you, and roll it up evenly, lightly pressing the third point to make it adhere to the roll; then bend the two ends towards each other in a crescent, or *croissant*, shape (Whence the name); bake ten to fifteen minutes in a rather quick oven. Brush each roll as you lift it out of the oven with egg yolk beaten up with a spoonful or two of milk. This makes them shiny, and prevents their hardening.[174]

Compare this to the American recipe given for a "Vienna crescent" on page 5, and then to this recipe from 1915, one of two offered by Sylvain Claudius Goy, a French cook who had long worked in America:

> No. 772. Croissants—A kilo of flour, 250 gr. of butter, 15 gr. of yeast, 15 gr. of salt, about 5 deciliters of milk.
>
> Make a leaven with a quarter of the flour, a little warm milk and the yeast. Let it rise to double its volume. Then make the dough by adding the rest of the flour, the salt, the milk and half of the butter. Let rise.
>
> Turn the dough out on the table. Roll it out with a rolling pin. Knead the remaining butter and spread it out in the center of the dough. Wrap. Give it four turns twice as for puff pastry. Let it sit for a good while.
>
> Roll the dough out to 8 millimeters thick. Cut it into small squares 4 or 5 centimeters on the side. Fold the corners of each into the center and mold them into little balls. Let sit. Powder them thickly with

flour. Roll out as for small pancakes. Butter half the surface with a brush. Then roll each circle on itself beginning by the unbuttered side. Set them as you go along on a lightly buttered cooking pan apart from each other forming small horseshoe-shaped rolls, the seam on top.

Let it rise until ready. Glaze. Cook in a hot oven.[175]

This is already a modern, puff-pastry based croissant, even if the recipe is somewhat perfunctory.

All evidence suggests that the puff-pastry croissant—the *croissant au beurre* —appeared early in the twentieth century.[176] The food historian Alan Davidson writes that the first "true" croissant recipe he found was from 1906, prompting him to conclude that the "history of the croissant, and its development into a national symbol of France, is a 20th century history." *N'exaggerons rien.*

Various references to croissant can be found all through the latter part of the nineteenth century. Aside from those listed earlier, here is an 1891 observation from *Le Gaulois*:

> Croissant of one sou and croissant of two sous, one cannot imagine the importance of this item in Parisian baking. An establishment in our neighborhood sells three to four thousand a day, and that just to customers off the street. Another, not so far away, sells over ten thousand of them. It is true that several local bakeries supply themselves there. [177]

Note too that the nineteenth century croissant came in two sizes, given by one source as weighing 36-37 and 60-80 grams.[178]

Henry James (1843-1916), recalling his childhood years in Paris under the Second Empire, speaks of the "so softly-crusty crescent rolls".[179] The date is vague, but would have preceded Dickens' 1872 mention (previously cited). In 1886, Mary Weatherbee recalled having "two crisp 'crescents' " for lunch when visiting Paris years before, while an English article from 1893 tells the reader to "butter a *croissant* or two".[180] Clearly the croissant was known early to travelers as one of the pleasures of France. Clearly, too, any changes made in the twentieth century were made to a pastry that had long been accepted as familiar, and French.

Still, the question arises: why, if French bakers knew of both puff pastry and the croissant, did it take so long to use the former for the latter?

It might be simply that it took some time for the pastry's "foreign" associations to wear off, inhibiting any conscious change in how it was made. But another answer lies in the then-standard use of puff pastry: an

1853 dictionary of food says: "Use it for vol-au-vents, dainty-dish tarts, little pâtés *au naturel*, tartlets, and for all light pastries, such as those with jam. Etc."[181] Puff pastry, in other words, was not typically eaten for its own sake, but was used to create shells or crusts to hold other preparations. (The one exception was the flat pastry known as a *galette feuilletée*, but even that does not seem to have been made with puff pastry until the latter half of the nineteenth century.) The remarkably successful idea of adding yeast to this dough and using it for a roll may have come in an instant, but it represented a radical, even inspired, change—especially since the croissant was already popular in its existing form.

What is more, as time went on not only the croissant but most viennoiserie has been made from puff pastry—that is, by a method invented in France. This has in effect "cut the cord" of "Vienna-style" products.

Today's viennoiserie is far more French than Viennese.

The Father of the Daily Vienna Press

IRONICALLY, ZANG'S GREATEST CAPITALIST SUCCESS grew directly out of the socialist stirrings of 1848.

It was at this point that Emile de Girardin, the publisher of *La Presse*, had a double effect on his friend's future. First of all, in the face of widespread unrest, he went, not as a newspaper owner, but as a deputy in the French legislature, to Louis-Phillipe and told him he must resign the throne.[182] The king did so, with results felt far beyond France.

In the ensuing upheaval, Zang returned to Vienna, where press censorship had been lifted for the first time in 58 years. Soon Girardin's influence on Zang would reveal itself in a far more direct way.

(The reader should bear in mind that the focus of this volume is on Zang's role in introducing viennoiserie and the croissant. What follows is only a brief survey of Zang's subsequent career. But both his success and his impact were enormous and any serious study of the man himself would linger far longer on points that here will only be noted in passing.)

"As of April in the year '48, there were already 70 new newspapers in Vienna". Today, reading about the Viennese press in this period recalls the Internet boom in America—a moment rich with possibility which attracted a motley assortment of entrepreneurs, not all of whom were qualified for the newest hot business. This might have been (and was) said of Zang himself, whose competitors would call him a "Kipfel-bake" (*Kipfelbäck*) and talk of the "effrontery" of this "Master-Baker" in speaking of "things not customary for one who scrapes a bread trough."[183]

Even less hostile writers, over time, could not resist underlining the connection:

> After the February revolution, M. Zang left Paris and returned to Vienna to found there, not now a bakery, but a newspaper, the Press. After bread for the body, bread for the spirit.[184]

> This same M. Zank [sic], after having founded... in Paris, the famous Viennese Bakery, came to Vienna to found a sort of intellectual bakery which had no less customers than the first.[185]

But as his competition would quickly learn, this "baker" was above all a savvy businessman and knew enough to surround himself with experienced journalists. More importantly, perhaps, he had carefully learned from Emile de Girardin.

Girardin

For well over a century readers of daily papers have taken several things for granted: that the paper would be cheap, even disposable; that it could be delivered to their door; that it would be supported by, and well furnished with, advertising. In early nineteenth century France, however, these were new concepts, and not without their critics.

Girardin, whom we have already seen criticized for his perceived cheapening of publishing, originated these and other ideas in France:

> To Girardin belongs the credit of having established a cheap daily press in France. Until 1836 the cheapest of the French dailies cost twenty and five-and-twenty centimes per copy, but that year Girardin... founded "La Presse", a daily political organ at the price of ten centimes, or a penny. Up to that time advertisements were almost unknown in French newspapers, but Girardin realized what a large source of revenue they might be made to yield, and it was on this point that he based his calculations.[186]

A visitor, having sketched Girardin's palatial home, wrote:

> He is celebrated as the inventor of new styles and of new papers—the cheap press in France, and the lilliputian paragraph were both the offspring of his brain. It would be hard to say which has been the more extensively copied, though perhaps the paragraph has the better claim to the distinction; for that, like the tricolor, seems to be making the tour of the world.

This writer then quotes an eight-line item—the journalistic equivalent of a sound bite—before continuing:

> It reminds one of the method of mincing food for babes and the infirm. An argument reduced to these proportions has been found digestible by the weakest minds; and when it is sold at a penny, it is in like manner within the resources of the slenderest purses. M. de Girardin has vulgarized political discussion in the least offensive sense.[187]

Zang had noted all this, as he had the financial and social benefits that accompanied Girardin's success. Already in Paris, he had begun to study the press business, even visiting Girardin's operation, as a decade before he had studied Viennese baking.

Die Presse

In the first days of May, Zang returned to Paris long enough to divest himself of his bakery. Did he sell it at a loss or, to the contrary, make his first fortune in Paris? Absent specific figures, it is impossible to say; a variety of sources give widely divergent, if equally assured, answers.[188]

Back in Vienna, after a first short-lived effort, he founded a second newspaper, and was not coy about copying his friend's methods.[189] When the new periodical appeared on Monday, July 3, 1848, it bore the same name as Girardin's *La Presse*, albeit in German: *Die Presse*.

> The large format was created in the image of the Paris *Presse*, it looked like a German edition of the Girardian journal: the editorials, the brief, set-off paragraphs, the daily news, the serials, the ads and announcements so cleverly ordered in narrow... columns that important things could be distinguished from the trivial..., and at the tip of the sheet the emblazoned invitation to subscribe, the laughably low price, made the paper a pleasure to buy. [190]

The new paper—bearing the motto "Equal Rights for All"—cost only 1 *kreuzer*, and offered free home delivery. The paper's success was immediate, and was to continue for some time. Baron von Helfert, a chronicler of Viennese journalism in 1848 and later a minister (1860-61), called it: "The most important journalistic creation of the year 1848, so in some sense of the whole new Austrian daily press in general."[191] Says a modern writer:

The first issue of Die Presse—July 3, 1848

Gathering round him an able group of associates, Zang attracted readers by pithy editorials and admirable articles on economic affairs. During the political reaction of the 1850's, the Presse was frequently in hot water with the censor; still it prospered and was spoken of as the most influential of Austrian papers.[192]

It would ultimately be noticed as far away as the United States:

> In 1848, a man appeared in Vienna who has entirely revolutionized journalism in the Austrian capital. This bold reformer, the father of the daily Vienna press of today, was neither a littérateur of extraordinary ability nor a poor journalist, favored by Fortune, but a baker, named August Zang.
>
> This man, while residing in Paris, where he did an excellent business with *Wiener Kipfeln* and *Kaisersemmeln* (different kinds of fine bread), had made himself as throughly acquainted as possible with the editorial and administrative departments of the Parisian journals. He took especial pains to study the system on which Emile Girardin conducted his paper, *La Presse*; and when, on his return to Vienna, he saw the condition journalism was in throughout the whole empire, he promptly decided to start a paper upon the Girardin plan. This he did in 1848, calling his paper *Die Presse*. The enterprise was exceedingly successful. The editorials of the new journal, the *feuilleton* —for which Zang secured some popular novels—and the discussions of economical and financial subjects, met with great favor. Zang directed both the business and editorial departments of his paper so cleverly that, in a comparatively short time, he became a millionaire.[193]

In 1885, a French writer, looking back at the paper's first years said, "The *Presse*, in its youth, had irresistible impulses, communicative enthusiasms, incendiary ardors."[194]

Not everyone admired Zang's approach. A writer in the original *La Presse* wrote in 1870 that Zang and his successors showed:

> The difference in the character of the periodical press in Paris and that of Vienna. In Paris an editor wants to become a politician, deputy and minister. In Vienna, he is concerned with business and with millions...[195]

This Austrian estimation from 1929 is exceptionally harsh:

> The one political journal in Vienna in these days, the Press, belonged to August Zang, a man who had assimilated the dubious characteristics of the new school of journalism in Paris under the Napoleonic regime, and in Austria was the father of press corruption in the modern sense. From this time, too, dates the evil connection

between this malleable semi-official press and the rapidly developing interests of international finance and its representatives in Vienna.[196]

In fairness, when similar accusations were made early in his paper's existence, Zang responded by printing a detailed budget to show he had nothing to hide.[197] But overall questions of the paper's worth and (sometimes rocky) relations with the government or other powers are beyond our scope here.

What no one disputes is that the new paper was an enormous success and made the "*Kipfelbäck*" very rich.

Zang, the Man

> To sketch the character of a man like Zang falls outside the scope of this work, and how public opinion judged him, we are reluctant to repeat.
>
> **Constant Von Wurzbach**[198]

Accounts of Zang typically speak far more of his activities than of his character. Further, the exceptions to this were written when he was already a prominent and powerful man and, whatever their slant, were unlikely to be neutral.

Yet Zang's character must have been of more than usual interest. He went from being a military man to running a fashionable bakery to managing an immensely successful and influential paper. This implies not only both ambition and vision, but an ability to flourish in very different worlds. He was unlikely, in a word, to have been a limited or inflexible man. Yet so he appears, at least in his later career. And before?

Richter paints an unflattering yet poignant picture of the young Zang. His prominent surgeon father was rejecting and harsh, while Zang himself:

> was no Apollo: his small stocky shape, the broad back, strong neck, a round face with a sharp and questioning glance, the ... almost misshapen turned up nose, did not make up a human form that inspired ... admiration ...; either in women or men. Zang did not make a good first impression.[199]

Richter writes that he had energy and ambition, and was "full of spirit, acumen and wit", but that "there was a strong streak of vanity at his core."

A modern reader might wonder, if his father's attitude and his own person were as described, how deep such "vanity" went.

By this account, even Zang's invention of a rifle was a (failed) attempt to make a name for himself, as were his efforts to fit in with the Viennese nobility. Later in life, he was "liberal, only in the sense that he could not overcome his anger over the failure of his role as a Cavalier." This same failure, Richter writes, prompted him to seek success in the less exalted domain of "the golden handicrafts".

One can barely glean from this portrait what qualities earned Zang the hand of a beautiful young woman from a good family. Presumably his "spirit, acumen and wit" played some part in that success.

Richter has less to say about the period that most interests us here, and the same French writers who praise Zang's bakery are silent about its owner. Given the establishment's popularity with people of distinction and the praise for its decor, it is tempting to deduce that Zang showed some modicum of charm and taste. But perhaps these too were skills he delegated.

Back in Vienna, and having become a press magnate, Zang seemed to revel in cheerfully crass comments. He apparently enjoyed being quoted as having said that "the day will come when the Queen of England will place her throne-speech as an ad in Die Presse."[200] Another much-repeated line was that his ideal would be "a newspaper that did not contain a single line that had not been paid."[201] (Did he know Samuel Johnson's "No man but a blockhead ever wrote but for money?") Yet another was worthy of a modern media tycoon: "My paper is a shop; I sell advertising."

Had he truly become so venal? At the least, these statements discount Zang's own talent as a journalist:

> It has often been said that Zang was a skilled businessman, but was not equipped to wield a pen, to write a good article. That is not true. Often, and on major occasions, Zang wrote articles and those in his hand were among the best, those which attracted the greatest interest.[202]

Did his mind narrow and coarsen as he became richer, more powerful and (not incidentally) older or did he to the contrary retain a youthful sense of mischief which prompted him to provoke?

No "Citizen Kane" was ever made about August Zang, but it might be instructive to compare his trajectory with that of its protagonist, or even of its model, William Randolph Hearst.

Now, when the mayor of Vienna called his face "grotesque" and "one of the most repulsive... under the sun,", he was not referring to its turned up nose, but to the "coarseness, arrogance, impertinence, malice and greed" it showed.[203]

A vivid, if certainly not neutral, portrait of the older Zang was left by the music critic Edward Hanslick, who worked for him for several years. Hanslick begins with something like admiration:

> The extraordinary expansion of his "Press" amply demonstrated Zang's rare administrative and financial talent, his single-minded tireless capacity for work. He represented the political mission of the newspaper with unflinching courage...

Then the tone begins to shift: "As he had a very pragmatic nature, art, science and fine literature did not exist for him." However, Hanslick adds that Zang's lack of interest in culture had the advantage that he did not, like other newspaper owners, pressure artists to perform for private affairs, lest they receive "ungracious" reviews. Zang, he says, simply did not care: "He was all business. His only ambition, his only pride was his newspaper, of whose influence and indispensability he had a great idea."

He goes on however to frankly criticize Zang on several points, notably his stinginess. Even after Hanslick extracted a raise from his very rich employer, he felt it was too little. Still, this was not his main complaint:

> It was not at all Zang's miserliness, it seems to me, that made the man perfectly distasteful, but his whole nature, which neither knew nor held any ideals, and only recognized the advertising side of the business. His small turned up nose with round nostrils gave his face a defiantly vulgar expression; no friendly glance ever fell from his bespectacled gray eyes, nor ever from his fleshy lips a kind word. I found the whole man so unpleasant that I avoided running into him. Throughout the years, I only spoke to him three or four times. Zang has a lot of money and very few friends left. [204]

Perhaps this is a fair portrait. Entrepreneurs are not always known for their people skills. But had the young officer, or the man who welcomed Parisian society, been equally off-putting?

After Die Presse

> Zang's stinginess became his last misfortune.
>
> **Eduard Hanslick**[205]

Hanslick is not the only one to blame Zang's "stinginess" for a fatal miscalculation. When two of his key employees asked for raises, he refused, and they left to found their own journal:

> September 1, 1864 saw the first issue of the "Neue Freie Presse." *Max Friedlaender* and *Michael Etienne*, the founders of the new sheet, had been the soul of August Zang's "Press". In his short-sighted stinginess Zang had let this soul escape, and we its other little souls happily flew after. The somewhat lengthy title of the new sheet stems from the fact that Zang, when he got wind of Friedländer's plan, immediately registered two of his projected new newspapers with the Government, titled: "New Press" and "Free Press". ..There remained only the more contrived, "New Free Press."[206]

(Several sources give this, erroneously, as the title of Zang's own paper, or say that he was involved with the new one.)

The site for Styria, the press group that owns the modern *Die Presse*, gives another explanation:

> In 1864 the editorial offices under Max Friedländer and Michael Etienne separated from founder Zang. In spite of large contributions at the beginning, Zang understood the needs of an independent quality newspaper less and less. He wanted to further his political and economical private interests through the paper. [207]

The new paper quickly caught on:

> The New Press soon supplanted the old, thanks to the skill, the real talent and the Yankee flair of M. Etienne. One could only be properly informed by reading this new paper, set up like the Times, and which kept day and night before its offices princely cars available to its editors and collaborators.[208]

Zang's publication was soon known as "the old Press".

> M. Zang, in despair, saw his circulation sink disastrously. He struggled with all his forces; but, as a good businessman, he understood that his sheet had become a bad deal and he got rid of it.[209]

On April 16, 1867, the original *"Press"* (in Paris) carried this brief item:

> Vienna, April 15
>
> A Prague businessman, M. Geiker, acting as the representative of several houses of commerce, several German, not Austrian, has just acquired the property of the Vienna paper the *Presse*, which belonged to M. Zang.[210]

This hardly left Zang idle. He had already founded "Concordia", a journalists' association, in 1859 and was involved in politics. He now became the head of a bank. In 1877, he established a handsome country seat in Styria at Schloss Greissenegg, a 13th century castle which remains a tourist attraction today. He also went into mining in the same region, opening the Voitsberg lignite mine.[211] (Its location is still called "Zangtal"— Zang Valley—today.)

"The Well-Bread Count"

How did Zang, having reached these exalted heights, feel about his first success, back in Paris? By one account, not proud:

> In regard to the Viennese bakery which has so well become a part of Parisian life..., I recall an amusing anecdote:
>
> Thirty years ago, a Viennese worker, without coin or trunk arrived in Paris—let us say in wooden shoes to not break with tradition—and went from being a bakery worker to being himself a boss; in the heart of Paris, near the Stock Market, he rapidly made with his Viennese bakery a colossal fortune; it was then new, the novelty was worth millions to him. He sold his business, retired to Vienna, went into the mine and banking businesses and finally today, is a great Austrian banker.
>
> But where this becomes amusing, is that he absolutely wanted, being an influential person in Vienna, to take his name off his shop; his successor in Paris refused this, setting conditions the other was unwilling to meet.... and that is why one can see in the heart of Paris, every day, in letters a foot high, on the carts of a Viennese bakery, morosely drawn by women, the name of a great financier of Vienna (Austria).[212]

When Zang died on March 4, 1888, *Die Presse*'s obituary said only that he had "stayed a long time in Paris." Clearly, his seminal role in French baking was not a point of pride. On March 8, even the *New York Times*, which had previously praised his bread, wrote simply that "August Zang, doyen of the Vienna journalists and founder of the Vienna *Presse*, is dead."[213]

Several regional American newspapers, however, ran the same item:

> Count Zang, who died in Vienna recently, made a fortune of $8,000,000 by the sale of Vienna bread. In 1842 he opened the first shop in Paris for the production of Vienna bread, and the bakery still exists on the Rue Richelieu under the name of the Maison Zang.

One of these had run an item just weeks before calling him "Herr Zang". Though he might have been pleased to be posthumously anointed "Count Zang", he probably would have been less pleased to see his considerable fortune ascribed to baking. Mercifully, most versions of the item omit one dubious claim, no doubt added by an anonymous wit: "Zang was sometimes spoken of as 'the well-bread count'."[214]

One offered his (much-distorted) model as an inspiration:

> Count Zang, of Vienna, made $8,000,000 by baking bread. The information is respectfully referred to those American wives and mothers who are putting in the time painting one legged storks on pickle jars.[215]

Despite his discreet obituary in *Die Presse*, even in Vienna some remembered Zang's role in baking. At the end of the century, when Emil Braun listed "Great Men Identified With the Baker's Trade", he only mentioned two fellow Austrians, one an actor who had started as a baker and the other Zang:

> August Zaug [*sic*], of Vienna, who was the founder and publisher of the *Wiener Presse*, one of the most influential newspapers in the stormy period of 1848, also laid the foundation of his fortune as a baker. He started the first Vienna bakery in Paris, baking all the popular Vienna rolls and specialties of the very best quality. His business grew rapidly and he soon became rich. After he sold out his interest in Paris at an enormous price, he returned to Vienna and devoted his time to newspaper and literary work.[216]

What, out of all he had done, did Zang himself take pride in? Above all, his newspaper; he was buried with a copy of *Die Presse* carrying his own obituary. Otherwise, he left an answer carved in stone; for even in death, Zang sought to impress.

In *A Short History of Art in Vienna* (2001), Martina Pippal describes his tomb, still shown to tourists today:

> Natter unites the Canova motifs [*of the Archduchess Maria Christina's tomb*] with late Romantic, Baroque and Antique features. The Egyptian-style doorway, tapering towards the top, is cut into a pyramidal rock. On either side of the entrance dwarfs hold miner's lamps in place of 'real' candles. The doorway would thus seem to lead not to the underworld, but to a mine-shaft -.... Canova's genius of death is replaced by a young man... In his right hand the young man grasps a broken chain and, with his left, supports a tablet bearing the inscription '*Die Presse/Motto: Gleiches Recht fur*

Alle/Gegrundet von August Zang 1848' (*Die Presse*/Motto: Equal Rights for All/Founded by August Zang, 1848.)[217]

But Zang also left a far more visible and widespread monument: today, after several interruptions and changes in ownership, hundreds of thousands of Austrians again read *Die Presse*, founded in 1848 by August Zang.

Meanwhile, Back in Paris...

BY THE TIME ZANG LEFT FRANCE IN 1848, "Viennese bakeries" were commonplace in Paris. But this not mean that the bread made there was the equal of that made in Vienna, anymore than most "French bread" made in America is comparable to that in Paris. When, in 1867, a "Viennese bakery" was set up at the Universal Exposition, with bakers, equipment and products direct from Vienna, it was a sensation: "People flock to taste the delicious rolls hot from the oven";[218] "The Parisian bakers are celebrated... for their fine bread; yet I am told that the produce of the Austrian bakery... has made them quite envious."[219] After the 1873 fair, in Vienna itself, the American government went so far as to produce a *Report on Vienna Bread*:

> It is known that efforts have been made to introduce the production of the Vienna bread to the public of other countries, but with indifferent success. The trained journeymen-bakers of Vienna are sought for and obtained to serve in other capitals; but the bread they produce is inferior.[220]

There were multiple reasons for this, among which an American commissioner mentioned the superior (and still expensive) Hungarian flour and "the Vienna system of baking, which unites to superior materials of all kinds an excessive care in all the manipulations of the baker."[221]

Still, all this could only have helped renew the popularity of Viennese baked goods. Forty years after Zang's departure, the original French *Presse* wrote that a "parallel" corporation of bakers existed, specialists in Vienna-style products, who charged no fixed rate, but negotiated each engagement: "A few Frenchmen have slipped into it, but most are Prussian or Austrian, but all claim to be Swiss or even Alsatian."[222] A report on the 1900 Universal Exposition said:

> Bakers who make luxury breads also employ 1,000 to 1,200 workers, called *Viennese*, who, for the most part, are from Austro-Hungary, German Switzerland, very few from France. They are paid

on average 10 to 14 francs a day; there are even some whose weekly salary reaches 100 francs, plus bread, like the French workers.[223]

And so the success of Vienna-style products, though not yet called "*viennoiserie*", continued. But how many of those who now ate them remembered that they had first appeared on the rue de Richelieu?

In the second half of the century, Baron Haussman had begun to expand and add to Paris' boulevards. Several were now as grand and tempting as General Mercer had found the Boulevard des Italiens. "A new shopping district arose to the north and west of the *grands boulevards* to supplement the older one around the Palais Royal and along the rue de Richelieu..."[224] To supplement, and soon to replace it; by 1874, an American writer called the street: "the once fashionable but now almost rococo Rue de Richelieu... fallen somewhat into the sear and leaf."[225] Its decline however was neither swift nor total. Eight years later, Charles Dickens, Jr. wrote that "some of the shops in the Rue de Richelieu are among the best in Paris, and as a rule they will be found at the end of the street nearest to the boulevard" (which is where the bakery was located). His biggest complaint was about the traffic: "The Rue de Richelieu is one of the most crowded streets in Paris. It is not, according to our present notions, a wide street, and the traffic is constantly increasing. A block caused by omnibuses, carts, and carriages will occur there as likely as in any other part of Paris." [226]

Rue de Richelieu (undated)

Staub died in 1852 and within a few years the building was owned, not by a fashionable tailor, but by an insurance company. Still, elegance and culture had not completely left the building. Other tenants still included a major music publisher and, in a nod to the street's fashionable history, the *Moniteur de la Mode*, which published patterns and descriptions of the latest fashions in both French and English. In 1860, the latter drew Isabella Beeton—most known for her book on household management—to the building to discuss the use of patterns in her own magazine.[227]

Though both neighborhood and neighbors were changing about it, the Boulangerie maintained its superior reputation for decades after Zang's departure—even if as illustrious a newspaper as the *New York Times* seems not to have noticed he *had* departed, at least not in 1855:

> Here competition produces its ordinary effect, and he who gives the largest quantity and the best quality for the money, is likely to obtain the heaviest business; as for instance, Mr. ZANG, of the Rue de Richelieu.[228]

An 1855 advertisement shows the owner then to have been "Parrod" and in 1860 Baedeker's guide recommended "*Parrot* [sic], *formerly Zang*, 'Pâtisserie Viennoise', rue Richelieu 92."[229] Fourteen years later, the same guide listed "Dubois" at the same address among the best "pâtissiers" and again through 1881.[230] (In 1870, when France was at war with Prussia, Jules Dubois contributed, along with some of his workers, to a patriotic subscription.[231] Given the Germanic origin of the bakery, they may have felt more need than most to show their loyalty.)

Though Baedeker's had dropped the address by 1884, the bakery's reputation remained strong. In 1886, Barbaret wrote: "Not only does it continue today, but it remains at the head, in terms of value, of Parisian bakers."[232] In 1895, Kerohant confirmed its continuing success: "This house still exists and prospers."[233]

The bakery came close to disaster one April night in 1888, when its chimney set the rafters on fire. But the local firemen, with a little help from a neighboring firehouse, quickly put it out.[234]

It is very unlikely that, even a few years after Zang left, most Parisians associated the bakery with the founder of a major Viennese daily. As it is, *Le Gaulois*, having published an (error-riddled) obituary in 1888 saying that "M[onsieur] Zang" had made money from his bakery, wrote only three years later that "Count Zang" had ruined himself in trying to improve the bakery and did not mention *Die Presse* at all.[235]

This would not be the last time Monsieur Zang the press magnate and Count Zang the luxury baker would be treated as two separate people, with a host of associated errors.

Still, if in fact Zang had tried to get his name removed from the business, he was monumentally unsuccessful. Over the years, even as it was listed under the names of various owners, the bakery continued to use Zang's name as well. Philibert Jacquet had bought the bakery by 1889, when "Zang, Boulangerie Viennoise (Jacquet, successor)" was one of four gold medal winners at the Universal Exposition.[236] The Eiffel Tower was built for that event and the *Figaro* set up a pavilion on its second platform, with a buffet provided by the *"boulangerie viennoise* Zang and Luncher". [237] In 1894, though Jacquet owned it then, an ad appeared for the "Zang bakery, 92, rue de Richelieu. Delivers morning and night rich bread and ordinary bread."[238] The bakery's historic address was still a point of pride as well; in 1896, Jacquet trademarked the "Richelieu 92 Roll", which was probably (no details survive) a type of Vienna roll.[239] Jacquet's was again chosen to represent France at the 1900 Universal Exposition.[240]

While it is not clear how long he owned the bakery, Jacquet's name, as will be seen, has endured.

In 1909, the bakery maintained Zang's custom of embossing his name on its products: "There is no elegant meal in which does not appear 'the Richelieu 92 Roll', this famous creation of Zang's whose brand is inscribed in its glazed crust...."[241]

But the bakery which had brought viennoiserie to Paris, and whose owner had jealously guarded the reputations of its products, now also claimed credit for another, very different, product, one still sold today: ready-made toast.

> Overstated reputations are not long in dying out, their length is their very justification. It is thus that, solidly established, the legitimate reputation of "Jacquet grilled bread" from the Zang establishment, 92, rue Richelieu, (Telephone 126-20), grows and is confirmed further each day.[242]

The bakery had produced this for some time. In 1891, in an unconscious echo of Moullet's earlier claims, an ad proclaimed:

> Twenty remedies have been offered one after the other against dyspepsia. There is none better and above all simpler than Jacquet's digestive grilled bread, which, in the opinion of all doctors, is the food best born by lazy stomachs. Made with particular care at the Boulangerie Viennoise, rue de Richelieu, 92, it leads to a good and easy digestion and one achieves a complete cure.[243]

In the twentieth century, similar items continued to appear, and one in 1912 warned of the falsification of "Jacquet grilled bread... which is only found at Zang's, rue Richelieu, 92."[244] Similar ads appeared in 1913 and 1914.

The bakery's later status is uncertain. In 1918, Henriette Boucquard, a baker at that address, was condemned for selling grilled bread despite wartime restrictions. The *Figaro's* item on this does not mention Zang's; yet in 1990 Calvel wrote that the bakery then still existed.[245] Certainly, today (2009) it is gone; a Spanish nightclub occupies the address. One former owner's name, however, has endured as the name of a modern corporation:

> Jacquet SA.... had its origins in a small, family-owned bakery opened by Philibert Jacquet in Paris in 1880. Jacquet invented a new type of toast, Pain Grillé, which he patented and marketed under the Jacquet brand. In 1946, the Jacquet company was bought up by Lucien Joulin. Under Joulin, Jacquet became the first in France to produce pre-sliced, packaged bread.[246]

Did Jacquet invent his bread at a "small, family-owned bakery" and then acquire the rue de Richelieu location? If so, this only confirms the prestige of that address in the late nineteenth century, even as the street around it declined.

Whatever the answer, it is ironic that toast became the bakery's most vaunted product. Even Zang's successors did not think to boast of what might fairly have been the establishment's greatest claim to fame: as the bakery that brought the croissant to Paris and helped make French bread what it is today.

NOTES

1. Georg Curtius, *Principles of Greek etymology*, trans. Augustus Samuel Wilkins, tr. Edwin Bourdieu, (London: J. Murray, 1886), II:146.
2. United States Commission to the Vienna exhibition, *Reports of the commissioners of the United States to the International Exhibition held at Vienna, 1873*, ed., Robert Henry Thurston (Govt. Print. Off., 1876), II:99.
3. Marcel Baudoin, "Croissant", *Intermédiare des Chercheurs et Curieux* XCVI,No. 1800, (November 30, 1933): 886-888.
4. *Mittheilungen der Kaiserl. Königl. Central-commission zur Erforschung und Erhaltung der Baudenkmale* (Vienna: K.K. Hof- und staatsdruckerei, 1869), XIV:vi.
5. Dr. Ferdinand Keller, "Benedictiones Ad Mensa Ekkehardi Monachi", *The Archaeological Journal* XXI (London: Office of the Institute, 1864) 352.
6. Jacob Grimm and Wilhelm Grimm, *Deutsches Wörterbuch von Jacob Grimm und Wilhelm Grimm* 11, 16 Vols. (Leipzig: S. Hirzel, 1854), 11:78; accessed April 6, 2009 on
http://germazope.uni-trier.de/Projects/WBB/woerterbuecher/dwb/wbgui?lemmode=lemmasearch&mode=hierarchy&textsize=600&onlist=&word=kipfel&lemid=GK05212&query_start=1&totalhits=0&textword=&locpattern=&textpattern=&lemmapattern=&verspattern=#GK05212L0
For Ennenchel's original text, see Hans Ennenchel, "Aus Ennenchels Reimchronik", in Georg Wolfgang, Karl Lochner, *Zeugnisse über das deutsche Mittelalter aus den deutschen Chroniken (*Nürnberg: Bauer and Raspe,1837), 54.
7. "Appalta per la fornitura del pane nel 1757", *Raccolta delle leggi, ordinanze e regolamenti speciali per Trieste* (Italy: 1861), 9.
8. See Pasquale Fornari, *Il Piccolo Carena* (Milan: Paoloa Carrara, 1875) 191 and Peschieri, *Dizionario Parmigiano-Italiano* (Borgo San Donnino:Giuseppe Vechhi, 1836) 274.
9. http://it.wikipedia.org/wiki/Croissant (Accessed July 17, 2009).
10. Bernard Clayton, *Bernard Clayton's New Complete Book of Bread* (New York: Simon & Schuster, 1973, 1983, 1995), 526.
11. S. Beaty-Pownall, *The "Queen" Cookery Books: No. 11. Bread, Cakes and Biscuits* (London: H. Cox, 1902), 51.
12. Ella Oswald, *German Cookery for the English Kitchen (*London : A. Siegle., 1906), 230.
13. Henriette Davidis, *Praktisches Kochbuch für die Deutschen in Amerika* (Milwaukee, Wisconsin: Geo. Brumder, 1897), 372.
14. Aliza Green, *Starting With Ingredients* (Philadelphia: Running Press, 2006) 782.
15. Davidson, 275.
16. J. Thompson Gill, *The Complete Bread, Cake and Cracker Baker in Two Parts*, (Chicago: J. Thompson Gill,, 1881), I:221, 222, 219.
17. G. Phillips Bevan,"Food Products", *Reports on the Vienna Universal Exhibition of 1873* Volume 73:Part IV (London: Eyre and Spottiswoode, 1874) 232.

NOTES

18 Friedrich Otto von Leber, *Rückblicke in deutsche Vorzeit: Die Ritterburgen Rauheneck, Scharfeneck und Rauhenstein mit geschichtlichen Andeutungen über die Vemgerichte und Turniere* (Vienna:Braumüller & Seidel, 1844) I:28; Curt V. Belau, "Küche und Keller im Wandel der Jahrhunderte", Erster Allgemeine Beamtenvereines der Österreichisch-Ungarischen Monarchie, *Die Dioskuren* (Vienna: C. Gerold's Sohn., 1888) XVII:44.

19 François Massialot, *Le nouveau cuisinier royal et bourgeois* (Paris: C. Prudhomme, 1734), III:258. Strangely, Zang's bakery produced *profiteroles* for soup in 1858, when they were already considered archaic ("Recettes du Gourmet", *Le Gourmet: journal des intérêts gastronomiques*, April 4, 1858).

20 Doug Lennox, *Now You Know Big Book of Answers 2* (Toronto: Dundurn Press Ltd., 2008) 317; "Some stories stem from the tale of the same Austrian bakers who conjured up Rugelach in celebration of victory over the Turkish siege of Vienna, hence the Turk's-head Kugelhopf mold. It's rumored that Marie Antoinette, an Austrian herself, brought the yeasted confection to France when she married Louis-Auguste." accessed on September 20, 2009 http://www.sugaredellipses.com/?p=379

21 Charles Dickens, "The Turks' Cellar", *Household Words: A Weekly Journal* X, No. 234 (September 16, 1854): X:114-115.

22 Henry Greenough, *Ernest Carroll, or Artist-life in Italy: A novel*, 2nd edition (Boston: Ticknor and Fields, 1858), 241.

23 Emil Braun, *The Baker's Book: a practical hand book of the baking industry in all countries*, trans. the author (New York: the author, 1902), II:334.

24 Karl August Schimmer, *The Sieges of Vienna by the Turks: Translated from the German of Karl August Schimmer and Others*, trans. Earl of Francis Egerton Ellesmere (London: John Murray, 1879), 30-31.

25 *Larousse Gastronomique*, ed. Prosper Montagne, Revised Edition (New York: Clarkson Potter, October 2, 2001), 372.

26 Edward Boucher James, *Letters, Archaeological and Historical: Relating to the Isle of Wight* (London: H. Frowde, 1896), 415.

27 Nicole Alper, Lynette Rohrer, Wild Women Association, Wild Women Association, *Wild Women in the Kitchen: 101 Rambunctious Recipes & 99 Tasty Tales*, (San Francisco:Red Wheel, 1996), 136.

28 Société des sciences morales, des lettres et des arts de Seine-et-Oise, *Mémoires de la Société des sciences morales, des lettres et des arts de Seine-et-Oise* V XVIII (Versailles: Marpon and Flammarion, 1893): 252.

29 Stéphanie Félicité de Genlis, *Manuel de Voyage à l'Usage des François en Allemagne* (Berlin: P. T. de Lagarde, 1799), 54-56.

30 Anselme Payen, "Etat de la Boulangerie dans la Grande-Bretagne", *Mémoires d'Agriculure, d'Economie Rurale et Domestique*, Paris, Bouchard-Huzard, 1850, 1er partie.

31 Anselme Payen, *Des substances alimentaires et des moyens de les améliorer, de les conserver et d'en reconnaître les altérations* (Paris: L. Hachette et Cie, 1853), 211.

32 Cited in Alan Davidson, *The Penguin Companion to Food*, Revised edition

NOTES

(Penguin (Non-Classics), October 29, 2002) 275.
33. Charles Dickens, "The Cupboard papers: VIII. The Sweet Art", *All the Year Round* 9, No. 209 (November 30, 1872): 61.
34. A. Ceriieux, "Les Gateaux et Bonbons Traditionnels", *Revue des Traditions Populaires* XII, No. 7 (July 1897), XII:372.
35. "The Vienna Press", Appleton's' *Journal of Literature, Science and Art* VII (Mar 23, 1872):VII:320.
36. For Zang senior's date of death, see Jean E. Dezeimeris, *Dictionnaire historique de la médecine ancienne et moderne* (Paris: Bechêt Jeune et Labbé, 1839), 429. Descriptions of August Zang's early years are primarily from H. M. Richter, "Die Wiener Presse", *Wien, 1848-1888*, (Vienna: Commission's Printer of Carl Konegen, 1888), II:536-545.
37. Dietmar Grieser, "Vom Backofen an den Reaktionsschreibtisch", *Die Presse*, (December 30, 1997):8.
38. Austro-Hungarian Monarchy K.u.K. Kriegsministerium, *Militär Schematismus des Österreichen Kaiserthumes*, (Vienna:k.k. Hof- und Staats-Druckerei, 1836), 268.
39. Hervé de Kerohant, "L'Alimentation de la France", *Le Correspondent* 67 (October 10, 1895):468.
40. Joseph Barbaret, *Le Travail en France: Monographies Professionelles I* (Paris: Berger-Levrault, 1886), I:385.
41. Grieser, 8; see also Günther Haller, "*Bei mir Müßte sogar die englische Königin ihre Thronrede inserierden*" *August Zang und seine "Presse"* in Julius Kainz and Andreas Unterberger, *Eine Stück Öesterreich: 150 Jahre Die Presse* (Vienna:1998, Verlag Holzhausen) and Richter, 537.
42. A. Merrick, "Bread and Yest [sic]", *The Gentleman's magazine*, Volume 86, Part 2, December 1862.
43. W. Scott Haine, *The history of France* (Greenwood Publishing Group, 2000), 102.
44. Richter, 537.
45. Adam Wandruszka, *Geschichte einer Zeitung: das Schicksal der "Presse" und der "Neuen freien Presse" von 1848 zur Zweiten Republik* (Vienna: Neue Wiener Presse Druck und Verlagsgesellschaft, 1958), 14.
46. Helmut Rumpler, Herwig Wolfram, *Eine Chance für Mitteleuropa: bürgerliche Emanzipation und Staatsverfall in der Habsburgermonarchie* (Vienna: Ueberreuter, 1997), 270.
47. *Biographie universelle ancienne et moderne : histoire par ordre alphabétique de la vie publique et privée de tous les hommes* XXXVIII, 85 vols., ed. Louis-Gabriel Michaud (Leiden, Michaud, 185?): 492.
48. "Germany", *La Presse* (September 29, 1848):NP (3).
49. Giles MacDonogh, "Reflections on the Third Meditation of *La Physiologie du goût* and Slow Food," *Slow Food Brillat-Savarin Paris-New York transatlantic meal* (September 24, 2005):8, www.slowfood.fr/bulletin/Diner_BS_PNY_2409_discours.pdf (accessed March 24, 2009)

NOTES

50 *La Presse* (December 6, 1839):NP (3).
51 Roman Uhl, "Brodbereitung", *Beiträge zur geschichte der gewerbe und erfindungen Oesterreichs: von der mitte des XVIII. jahrhunderts bis zur gegenwart*, ed. Wilhelm Franz Exner, (Vienna:W. Braumüller, 1873) II: 183.
52 Eugène Romain Thirion, "Le bon ton, Paris Rue de Richelieu, 92", image on NYPL Digital Gallery at http://digitalgallery.nypl.org/nypldigital/id?804083 (accessed March 24, 2009).
53 General Cavalié Mercer, *Journal of the Waterloo Campaign Kept Throughout the Campaign of 1815* (Edinburgh and London:William Blackwood and Sons, 1870) II:136-137.
54 Thomas Frognall Dibdin, *A Bibliographical Antiquarian and Picturesque Tour in France and Germany* (London:W. Bulmer and W. Nicol, 1821) II:93.
55 Louis Lurine, *Les Rues de Paris: Paris Ancien et Moderne* (Paris:G. Kugelmann, 1844) II:370.
56 F. Hervé, *How to enjoy Paris in 1842 intended to serve as a companion* (Paris: Amyot, 1842), 107.
57 Edward Planta, *A New Picture of Paris; or, the Stranger's Guide to the French Metropolis* (London:Samuel Leigh, 27) 439.
58 http://www.historicfood.com/Ice%20Cream%20Cone.htm (accessed July 22, 2009).
59 Ernest Feydeau, *Le rétablissement des jeux publics en France* (Paris: Noblet, 1871) 21.
60 Charles Lefeuve, *Les Anciennes Maisons de Paris: Histoire de Paris, rue par rue, maison par maison* (Paris:C. Reinwald and Co., 1875) V:334.
61 William Cullen Bryant, *Letters of a traveller: or, Notes of things seen in Europe and America* (London: Bentley, 1850) 220.
62 "Le Démon de Jeu," Le Magasin Pittorresque 80th year, Series II Vol. 13, 1912.
63 Alexandre Dumas, "Filles", *La Grande Ville* (Paris: Bureau Central des Publications Nouvelles, 1842) II:320-321.
64 Jules Janin, *Un Hiver a Paris,* 2nd ed. (Paris:L. Curmer, 1844) 45.
65 N. Parker WIllis, *Pencillings by the Way* (New York: Charles Scribner, 1860), 118.
66 Honoré de Balzac, *Le Diable a Paris* (Paris:Michel Lévy frères, 1857) 255-256.
67 Peter Bloom, *The Cambridge companion to Berlioz* (Cambridge University Press, 2000) 236, 280.
68 Auguste Vitu, *La Maison Mortuaire de Molière* (Paris:Alphonse Lemerre, 1883) 112, 248-249.
69 Henri Martineau, *L'oeuvre de Stendhal: histoire de ses livres et de sa pensée* (A. Michel, 1966) 522.
70 A Man on the Shady Side of Fifty, "France and Paris Forty, Thirty, and Twenty Years ago", *Fraser's Magazine for Town and Country*, Vol. LXII, No CCCLXXI, November 1860.
71 *Almanach des 25000 adresses des principaux habitans de Paris* (Paris:

NOTES

Panckoucke, 1835), 420.
72 Dupeuty, F. De Courcy and Maurice Alhoy, "Le Magasin Pittoresque", revue en quinze livraisons", *Le Magasin Théatral*, 1st year (Paris:Marchant, 1834) I:6 Scene III.
73 M. Leblanc, *Manuel du Pâtissier et de la Pâtisserie*, 2nd ed. (Paris:Roret, 1834) 263; Méry, *La Guerre du Nizam* (Paris: Victor Magen, 1847), III:100.
74 *Exposition de 1834, sur la Place de la Concorde: Notice des Produits de L'Industrie Française* (Paris: Everat, 1834) 100.
75 Girardin, "La Littérature à Six sous", *Revue de Paris* VIII, ed. Louis Désiré Véron, ed. H. Dumont, Brussels (Slatkine Reprints), (August 1834):VIII:204.
76 F. Lemaistre, *Paris En Miniature: Guide Pittoresque du Voyageur* (Paris: Garnier, 1856) 34.
77 Jean Anthelme Brillat-Savarin, *Physiologie du goût: ou, Méditations de gastronomie transcendante* (Paris: Charpentier, 1838) 263, 478. "Regulated breads" were ordinary breads; the prices of "luxury breads" (fancy breads) were not regulated.
78 C. B. D. M. "Horticulture: Sociétéd'Horticulture de Paris. Deuxième séance publique annuelle, tenue le dimanche 8 november 1829", *Bulletin des Sciences Agricoles et Economiques*, V. XIII (Paris: Firmin Didot, 1829).
79 *La France Littéraire*, 2nd Series (Paris:Offices of La France Littéraire, 1837) IV:345.
80 Oneddy Vitreuil,"Nocturne a plusieurs voix", *Le Pays de Breda* (Paris: Michel Lévy Frères, 1853) 85.
81 Constant von Wurzbach, *Biographisches Lexikon des Kaiserthums Oesterreich,* (Vienna: Bruch und Verlag der k. k. Gof- und Staatsbruckerei, 1890), 162.
82 MacDonogh, 8.
83 "Modes", *La Presse,* (November 12, 1839):NP (3).
84 Adolphe Boschot, *Un romantique sous Louis-Philippe,* 3rd edition (Paris: Plon-Nourrit, 1908), 504.
85 Viscount Charles De Launay [Delphine Gay de Girardin], "Courier de Paris", *La Presse*, (November 23, 1839):NP (2).
86 Sainte-Beuve, November 17,1839, "Une Correspondance Inédite de Sainte-Beuve - Lettres à M. et Mme Juste Oliver, troisième partie", *Revue des deux mondes* 18, (1903):18:310.
87 Une Société de Littérateurs, d'Archéologues et d'Artistes, *Paris Illustré* (Paris: L. Hachette et cie, 1855) 688.
88 Freihern von Reichenbach, "Ueber die Röstung orgnischer Körper", *Annalen der Chemie und Pharmacie* (Heidelberg: C. F. Winter, 1844) XLIX:16.
89 Bevan, 232-233.
90 "Etablissemens et magasins en vogue", *La Presse* (December 22, 1839):NP (3).
91 Willis, 72.
92 Gérard de Nerval, "Les Nuits d'Octobre", *La Bohème Galante* (Paris:Calman Levy, 1882) 189.

NOTES

93 "Liste des Membres de la Societe admis pendant l'annee 1840", *Bulletin de la Societe d'Encouragement pour L'Industrie Nationale* 39th year, December 1840.
94 Haller, 27.
95 "Bäckerei der Herren Gebrüder Mouchot zu Petit-Mont-rouge nächst Paris", *Allgemeine Bauzeitung mit Ubbildungen,* 1840.
96 "The Paris Baker", *Chambers' Edinburgh Journal* VII, No. 172, (April 17, 1847): 254.
97 "Demandes et Offres", *La Presse,* January 14, 1846.
98 "Recettes du Gourmet", *Le Gourmet: journal des intérêts gastronomiques,* April 4, 1858.
99 August Widal, "Un mois de séjour à Vienne", *Revue Germanique* 13, (1861): 80.
100 Théophile Gautier, *Voyage en Russie* (Paris:Charpentier, 1867), 188.
101 Théodore de Banville, "Credo", *Critiques,* ed. Victor Barrucand (Paris: Charpentier, 1917) 460-461.
102 "Nouvelles de Paris", *La Presse,* (January 1, 1852):NP (2).
103 *Bulletin des lois du Royaume de France* 25, IX series , No. 945, (August 1, 1842):XXV:232.
104 *Bulletin des Lois du Royaume de France* IX series, No. 1029, (April 12, 1843) XXVII:238.
105 Wandruszka, 15.
106 Anselme Payen, Jules Rossignon, J.-Jules Garnie, *Manuel du cours de chimie organique: appliquée aux arts industriels et agricoles* (Paris:N. Béchet Fils, 1842), 312-313.
107 Anselme Payen, *Précis de chimie industrielle à l'usage des écoles préparatoires aux professions industrielles des fabricants et des agriculteurs,* 2nd ed., (Paris:Hachette et cie, 1851), 456.
108 John Blandy, *The Baker's Guide and Practical Assistant to the Art of Bread-Making in All Its Branches* (London:Newton & Eskell, 1899), 140.
109 *Cosmos: revue encyclopédique hebdomadaire des progrès des sciences et de leurs applications aux arts et à l'industrie,* 1st year, (Paris: Salles de Cosmos, 1852), I:416.
110 Baron L. Brisse, *Album de l'Exposition Universelle* (Paris:Bureaux de L'Abeille Impériale, 1857) 392.
111 Michel Chevalier, *Rapports du Jury international, Tome Onzième: Groupe VII – Classes 67 a 73* (Paris: Dupont, 1868) 91.
112 France, Ministère de la marine et des colonies, *La Marine à l'Exposition universelle de 1878* (Paris, Gauthier-Villars, 1879) I:358-9.
113 See http://www.gastronomica.be/fr/pg/pg-005_3_21.html and http://fr.wikipedia.org/wiki/Pain (both accessed March 31, 2009).
114 Vallot, *Journal de la santé du roi Louis XIV de l'année 1657 a l'année 1711* (Paris: Durand, 1862), 208.
115 Pierre Jaubert, *Dictionnaire Raisonné Universel des Arts et Métiers: contenant l'Histoire, la Description, la Police des Fabriques et Manufactures*

NOTES

    de France et des Pays étrangers : ouvrage utile a tous les citoyens I, 5 vols. (Paris:P. Fr. Didot le jeune, 1773), I:350
116 "The Food of Paris", *the New Monthly Magazine VCVII*, No. 425, (June 1856):VCVII:166.
117 Raymond Calvel, *The Taste of Bread: A Translation of Le Goût Du Pain, Comment Le Préserver, Comment Le Retrouver*, trans. Ronald L. Wirtz, (Gaithersberg, Md: Aspen, 2001):116.
118 Benoit, Julia de Fontenelle, *Manuel Complet du Boulanger, du Meunier, du Négociant en Grains, et du Constructeur de Moulins* (Paris: Encyclopédie Roret, 1836) II:253-254.
119 J. Fontenelle and F. Malepeyre, *Manuels-Roret: Nouveau manuel complet du boulanger* (Paris:Encyclopédie Roret, 1871) 218-219.
120 Karel Kulp, Klaus J. Lorenz, *Handbook of dough fermentations* (New York:Marcel Dekker, 2003) 13.
121 "When a *poolish* is used as a pre-ferment it is usually, but not always, necessary to add more yeast during the mixing of the final dough to complete the leavening.... A regular sponge... is usually faster than a *poolish* because it front-loads all or most of the yeast in the sponge itself."; Peter Reinhart, Ron Manville, T*he bread baker's apprentice: mastering the art of extraordinary bread* (Berkeley: Ten Speed Press, 2001) 53.
122 Paul-Jacques Malouin, *Descriptions des Arts et Métiers* (Neuchatel: Société Typographique printer, 1771) I:205.
123 Léon Boutroux, *Le Pain et la Panification* (Paris: J.-B Baillière et fils:1897) 288-290.
124 Paul Richards, *Baker's Bread*, 4th edition (Chicago:the Bakers' Helper Company, 1918) 46.
125 From an unidentified periodical, commenting on the Vienna Exposition of 1873, quoted by François Malepeyre in the *Nouveau manuel complet du fabricant de levure: traitant de sa composition chimique, de sa production et de son emploi principalement dans la brasserie, la distillation, la boulangerie, la pâtisserie, l'amidonnerie et la papeterie* (Paris: Librairie Encyclopédique de Roret, 1875), 210.
126 Emil Braun, II:332-333.
127 *La Presse,* (December 14, 1841):NP (4) (advertisement).
128 MacDonogh, 8.
129 *Dictionnaire de la conversation et de la lecture: inventaire raisonné des notions générales les plus indispensables à tous, par une société de savants et de gens de lettres* 14, ed. M. W. Duckett (Paris: Aux comptoirs de la direction, 1853-1860), 14:99.
130 Barbaret, 384.
131 *La Presse* (February 12, 1840):NP (4) (advertisement).
132 Alexis de Valon, "La côte orientale de la Sicile", *Revue de Paris* V (May 1845):V:77.
133 Braun, I:17, and *Encyclopédie méthodique ou par ordre de matières* I, (Paris: Panckoucke, 1782), I:267.

NOTES

134 "Art. 224. Boulanger, Marque, Contravention, Amende, Cumul, Excuse, Force Majeure, Expertise", *Journal des justices de paix et des tribunaux de simple police. Recueil mensuel de législation, de jurisprudence et de doctrine*, ed. Charles Bioche (Paris:1852).
135 Caius, "Notes by the Road No. 11: How One Lives In Paris", *The American Whig Review*, (Oct. 1846):IV:383.
136 Louis Claude Joseph Florence Desnoyers, *Les étrangers à Paris* (Paris: C. Warée, 1846), 165.
137 Hervé de Kerohant, "L'Alimentation de la France: I - Le Pain", *Le Correspondant* 181 (new series 145), (November 10, 1895):CLXXXI:458.
138 Barbaret, I:385.
139 Francis Marre, "L'Industrie Laitière", *Le Correspondant* 229 (new series 193), (October 10, 1907):V229:170.
140 A. Bitard, *Le monde des merveilles: tableau pittoresque des grands phénomènes de la nature et des manifestations du génie de l'homme dans les sciences, l'industrie et les arts*, First Part (Paris: Librarie illustrée, 1878) 558.
141 Théodore Faullain de Banville, *Les belles poupées* (Paris: G. Charpentier, 1888), 270.
142 "Faits Divers", *La Semaine judiciaire: Journal des Tribunaux* 43, 6th year, (October 27, 1884):688.
143 Gaspard de Pons, *Adieux Poétiques suivis de Fatras Rimé* (Paris:Librairie Nouvelle, 1860) III:249.
144 "Les Boutiques de Paris", *Le Magasin Pittoresque* 12th, 1844 42-43.
145 A. Fayeux, "Un Nouveau Livre de Métiers", *La Science sociale suivant la méthode de F. Le Play*, 2nd year (Paris:Firman-Didot. 1887) IV:340-342.
146 "La Corporation des Ouvriers Boulangers au Public Parisien" (March 1872), quoted in Barbaret, 453.
147 *Michelin Red Guide 2008 Paris: Restaurants & Hotels* (Michelin Red Guide: Paris) (Michelin Travel Publications, April 2008) 231.
148 Much of what follow is excerpted from my own on-line paper "About the Baguette" (http://www.chezjim.com/books/baguette). Those interested in the bread itself may want to visit that URL.
149 Gilles Pudlowski, Maurice Rougemont, *Les trésors gourmands de la France* (Belgium:Renaissance Du Livre, 2000) NP.
150 Wells, October 9, 1983.
151 Emil Braun, *The baker's book: a practical hand book of the baking industry in all countries* (New York:E. Braun, 1902) II:335.
152 *Impressions and Observations of a Young Person During a Residence in Paris*, 2nd edition, quoted in "Notices of New Works", *The Metropolitan*, August, 1844.
153 A. Payen, *Précis de chimie industrielle* (Paris:Hachette, 1867) II:209.
154 Payen, II:210.
155 "Croissant, Brioches et Pain de Luxe", *Le Gaulois*, June 27, 1891.
156 "Le Prix du Pain", *La Presse* September 3, 1897.

NOTES

157 Raymond Calvel, Ronald L. Wirtz, James J. MacGuire, *The Taste of Bread: A Translation of Le Goût Du Pain, Comment Le Préserver, Comment Le Retrouver,* ed. James J. MacGuire, tr. Ronald L. Wirtz (Springer, 2001,) 116.
158 "Baguette is a foreign pain, says queen of French bread", *the Times,* June 25, 2007. http://www.timesonline.co.uk/tol/news/world/europe/article1980288.ece (accessed July 4, 2009).
159 Richards, 46.
160 "French bread abroad. Sold with an American accent," *The Economist,* U.S. Edition (September 27, 1997):97.
161 Husson, 78-79; Proceedings of Committee of Maintenance, session of December 21, 1812, quoted in Husson, 103.
162 "Bread for Parisian Poor", *The New York Times,* November 10, 1884.
163 *Le Figaro,* February 8, 1925, "La baisse du prix du pain", *Journal des Débats,* February 9, 1922; and Frederick Clampette, "Sad Hoptimists", *New Outlook,* December 6, 1922.
164 Schirmaker, *La spécialisation du travail par nationalités à Paris* (Paris:Arthur Rousseau, 1908) 102.
165 David, 362.
166 "The Paris Baker", *Chamber's Edinburgh Journal (*April 17, 1847):254.
167 Otto Maas, "Vienna Bread", *Logansport Journal,* August 4, 1880.
168 Henry Chastrey, 256. This article only notes the change to condemn it, pointing out (as many would agree today) that the old dark bread was far healthier and more nutritious. Such protests appear almost almost from the start of the popularity of white bread.
169 La Varenne, *Le Cuisinier François,* 11th ed. (Lyon: Jacques Canier, 1680), 170-171.
170 Payen, *Des substances alimentaires,* 211.
171 Barbaret, I:380.
172 Kerohant, CLXXXI:458.
173 Pierre Guichard, *Traité de distillerie: Industrie de la Distillation - Levures et Alcools,* (Paris:J.B. Baillière et fils, 1897), 340.
174 S. Beaty-Pownall, *the "Queen" Cookery Books: No. 11 Bread, Cakes and Biscuits* (London:Horace Cox, 1902) 51.
175 Sylvain Claudius.Goy, *La cuisine anglo - américaine, comprenant la cuisine anglaise, la cuisine américaine ... etc., précédée d'un petit historique de l'agriculture et des produits du Nouveau Monde au moment de sa découverte. La cuisine de l'Amérique Centrale, comprenant tous les plats de quelque importance usités dans ces contrées ...* (New York: L. Weiss & co., 1915), 95.
176 Used at the start of the century, the term is ambivalent, since it can also refer to any buttered croissant. A writer in 1901 speaks of "M. Jean- Marie-Gabriel Cretaine, baker, rue Dauphine, whose croissants au beurre were famous, forty years ago". (Henri Baillière, *La rue Hautefeuille : son histoire et ses habitants, propriétaires.et locataires* (1252-1901) (Paris:J.-B. Baillière,1901) 226). In 1861, the croissant was still more like the kipfel, and this appears to refer, simply, to a buttered croissant.

NOTES

177 *Le Gaulois*, June 27, 1891.
178 Armengaud père, « Boulangerie: Améliorations dans les procédés de fabrication », *Publication industrielle des machines, outils et appareils* v. 27, 2nd series (Paris:Librairie Téchnologique Armengaud Ainé, 1881) VII:509.
179 Henry James, *A Small Boy and Others* (London:Macmillan, 1913), 349.
180 Mary Weatherbee, "Europe on Nothing-Certain a Year", *The Century Illustrated Monthly Magazine* XXXII (new series Vol. X), Issue 6 (Oct. 1886):XXXII:939 and "The Economies of the Rich", quoted from *The Globe* in *The Living Age*, (April 1893):CXCVII:125.
181 *Dictionnaire général de la cuisine française ancienne et moderne ainsi que de l'office et de la pharmacie domestique* (Paris:Plon frères, 1853), 36.
182 Imbert de Saint-Amand, *The Revolution of 1848: With Portraits,* trans. Elizabeth Gilbert Martin, (New York: Charles Scribner's, 1895), 202-203.
183 Günther Haller, 21.
184 *PARIS guide; par les principaux écrivains et artistes de la France* (Paris: Librairie Nationale, 1867), 115.9.
185 Widal, *Revue Germanique*, VII:80.
186 Henry Vizetelly, *Glances Back Through Seventy Years: Autobiographical and Other Reminiscences* (London: Kegan Paul, Trench, Trubner & Co., Ltd, 1893), II:321.
187 Edmund Hodgson Yates, *Celebrities at Home: Reprinted from "The World"*, Third Series, (London: Office of 'The World', 1879), 123-124.
188 "His Viennese Bakery which lost him a good piece of money", Ernst Viktor Zenker, *Geschichte der Journalistik in Oesterreich* 43; "He made a fortune with his "boulangerie viennoise", *Austriaca*, Issues 32-35 (Rouen: Université de Rouen, Centre d'études et de recherches autrichiennes, 1991) 76.
189 Constant Von Wurzbach, *Biographisches Lexikon des Kaiserthums Oesterreich* (Vienna:Druck und Verlag der k. k. Gof—und Staatsdruckerei, 1890), LIX:163-164.
190 Richter, 539-540.
191 Erich Witzmann, "Nur "Die Presse" überlebte" http://diepresse.com/unternehmen/160jahre/395575/index.do?_vl_backlink=/unternehmen/160jahre/index.do (accessed April 8, 2009). (Print version August 3,.2008).
192 J Arthur May, *Hapsburg Monarchy* (New York:W. W. Norton and Company, Inc. September 17, 1968), 95.
193 "The Vienna Press", Appleton's' *Journal of Literature, Science and Art*, VII:320.
194 Paul Vasili, "La Société de Vienne", *La Nouvelle Revue* 32 (Jan.-Feb. 1885):32:471-472.
195 "Nouvelles Étrangères", *La Presse* (March 10, 1870):NP (3).
196 Joseph Redlich, *Emperor Francis Joseph Of Austria - A Biography* (New York: Macmillan, 1929), 244.
197 Haller, 23.
198 Wurzbach, LIX:165.

NOTES

199 Richter, 536.
200 Haller, 27.
201 Edward Timms, *Karl Kraus, Apocalyptic Satirist: Apocalyptic Satirist: Culture and Catastrophe in Hapsburg Vienna*, Edition: reprint, (New Haven:Yale University Press, 1989), 32.
202 Richter, 342.
203 Haller, 27.
204 Eduard Hanslick, *Aus Meinen Leben* (Berlin: Allgemeiner Verein für Deutsche Litteratur, 1894), 148-149; digitized on http://www.zeno.org/Kulturgeschichte/M/Hanslick, +Eduard/Aus+meinem+Leben/Achtes+Buch/1.?hl=zang+hanslick (accessed April 8. 2009).
205 Hanslick, 148.
206 Hanslick, 279.
207 http://www.ok-zeitung.at/en/konzernunternehmen/subpage.php?&cat=1&tochter=2&PHPSESSID=f6b0fa9820d8e79d312e921285a118ab&sub=3&PHPSESSID=f6b0fa9820d8e79d312e921285a118ab (accessed July 16, 2009).
208 Victor Tissot, *Vienne et la Vie Viennoise* (Paris:E. Dentu, 1878) 211-212.
209 Paul Vasili, *La Nouvelle Revue*, 471-472.
210 "Dépéches Télégraphiques", *La Presse* (April 16, 1867): NP (1).
211 Dietmar Grieser, "Vom Backofen an den Reaktionsschreibtisch", *Die Presse* (December 30, 1997):8.
212 Paul Vibert, *La concurrence étrangère: thémes de conférences* (Paris: Charles Bayle, 1887):48.
213 "Obituary Notes", *the New York Times (*March 6, 1888).
214 The *Evening Gazette,* Cedar Rapids, Iowa , included this line in the item on April 20, 1888; on April 5, the paper had referred to him as "Herr Zang". The *Atlanta Constitution,* (May 11) and the *Logansport Pharos* (April 20) were only two of the others that carried the shorter version.
215 *San Antonio Daily Express*, April 20, 1888.
216 Braun, I:32.
217 Martina Pippal, *A Short History of Art in Vienna* (Munich: C.H. Beck, 2001),164
218 L. de Hegermann-Lindencrone, *In the Courts of Memory* (Garden City, NY: Harper, 1911, 1912) 154.
219 "Paris and at its Exhibition of 1867", *British Farmer's Magazine* Vol. LIII, 1867 "Textless Notes by a Crotchety Farmer".
220 E. N. Horsford, *Report on Vienna Bread* (Washington: Government Printing office, 1875) 1.
221 United States Commission to the Paris Universal exhibition, *Reports of the commissioners of the United States to the Paris Universal Exhibition*, 1867 ed., William P. Blake (Govt. Print. Off., 1870), V:12.
222 "Paris Qui Travaille—les Boulangers", *La Presse* (February 6, 1885):NP (6).
223 Ministère du commerce, de l'industrie et des colonies Picard, Exposition

NOTES

universelle internationale de 1889 à Paris. *Rapports du jury international - Groupe VII. - Produits alimentaires (1re partie) Classes 67 à 73* (1st part) ed. Alfred (Paris: National Printer, 1891) 53.

224 Lenard R Berlanstein, *Big business and industrial conflict in nineteenth-century France: a social history of the Parisian Gas Company* (Berkeley/LosAngeles/London: University of California Press, 1991), 16.

225 Lucy H. Hooper, "Parisian Shops and Shopping", *Appleton's Journal of Literature, Science and Art* No 264, April 11, 1874.

226 Dickens, "Rue de Richelieu" *Dickens's Dictionary of Paris, 1882: an unconventional handbook* (London:MacMillan & Co, 1882) 221.

227 Alison Adburgham, *Shops and shopping, 1800-1914: where, and in what manner the well-dressed Englishwoman bought her clothes* (Allen and Unwin, 1964) 118 and Kathryn Hughes, *The short life and long times of Mrs. Beeton*, (New York:Knopf, 2006) 260.

228 "PARISIAN GOSSIP", *New York Times*, September 12, 1855.

229 M. T. Faucon, *Veritable Guide Parisien Pour les Étrangers* (Paris:Coulin-Pineau, 1855), NP; Karl Baedeker, *Paris, Rouen, Havre, Dieppe, Boulogne und die drei Eisenbahn-Strassen vom Rhein bis Paris. Handbuch für Reisende von K. Baedeker*, Edition: 3 (Leipzig: Karl Baedeker, 1860), 19.

230 K, Baedeker, *Paris and its Environs with routes from London to Paris, and from Paris to the Rhine and Switzerland*, 6th ed. (Leipzig: Karl Baedeker, 1874), 19. The same name appears in 1878 (Baedeker's, 24) and 1881 (17); there is no mention in 1884 (19).

231 "Souscription Patriotique", *Le Gaulois*, August 10, 1870.

232 Barbaret, *le Travail en France* Vol. I (Paris: Berger-Levrault, 1886), 385.

233 Kerohant, 458.

234 "Commencement d'Incendie", *Le Gaulois*, April 21, 1888. Students of Parisian history and/or firehouses might like to know that the local firehouse was "of the Library" (that is, the National Library, on the same street) and was helped by another from "Jean-Jacques Rousseau", presumably from the neighborhood which includes that sreet.

235 "Echoes de L'Etranger", *Le Gaulois*, March 7, 1888 and "Bloc-Notes Parisien: Croissants, Brioche et Pains de Luxe", *Le Gaulois*, June 27, 1891.

236 France. Ministère du commerce, de l'industrie et des colonies, *Exposition universelle. Paris. 1889. Rapports du jury international- Groupe VII. - Produits alimentaires (1re partie) Classes 67 à 73 (1re partie)*, ed. Alfred Picard, (Paris: Imprimerie nationale, 1891), 55; "Exposition Universelle de 1900: Produits de la Boulangerie et de la Patisserie", *Touring-Club de France, Rapports du Jury International: Groupe X - Aliments* (Paris:Imprimerie nationale, 1902), 275. These reports include useful histories of French baking.

237 *L'Universelle exposition de 1889 illustrée*, 3rd series, n° 1, dir. Alfred Le Roy (Paris: 1886-1888), 7.

238 *Le Gaulois*, June 26, 1894.

239 *Revue des vins et liqueurs et des produits alimentaires pour l'exportation*

NOTES

(Paris, 1896) 325.
240 Touring-Club de France, "Exposition Universelle de 1900: Produits de la Boulangerie et de la Patisserie".
241 "Informations", *Le Figaro* (Tuesday, November 9, 1909):5.
242 "Les Solides Reputations", *Le Figaro* (Tuesday ,February 2, 1909):4.
243 *Le Gaulois,* December 20, 1891.
244 "Falsifications", *Le Figaro* (Sunday, April 7, 1912):4.
245 "Gazette des Tribunaux", *Le Figaro* (Sunday, May 7, 1918): 3.
246 M. Cohen, "Groupe Limagrain", International Directory of Company Histories , Volume 74 (2003), available on http://findarticles.com/p/articles/mi_gx5202/is_2003/ai_n19123272/pg_2/ (accessed April 9, 2009).

Made in the USA
Lexington, KY
18 September 2010